Sport Optics

Binoculars, Spotting Scopes, and Riflescopes

Alan R. Hale

I apologize for any errors that may appear in this book. I have gone over the material many times and have had several others edit the material, but I cannot guarantee everything is 100% accurate and accept no liability for errors. I express many opinions in this book and that is what they are – my opinions.

Disclaimer for Astronomical Images: Amateur astronomers who used astronomical telescopes, various astronomical cameras and accessories supplied the deep sky, planetary and lunar images in this book. The images do not represent what you can see with binoculars and spotting scopes, and the details shown in the images. You will view deep sky astronomical objects in black and white color.

Published by Hale Optics
904 Silver Spur Road, # 191
Rolling Hills Estates, CA90274
www.haleoptics.com

ISBN 978-0-9897916-0-1

Library of Congress Cataloging-in-Publication Data is available on file.

Front Cover Images from left to right – Courtesy of Swarovski, Leica, and Zeiss

Printed in China

Acknowledgements

One thing gave me some enthusiasm to write an optics book. Earlier this year I purchased a book authored by Brin Best from the UK titled *Binoculars and People.* The book did not contain a lot of information about optics but it was a unique history of binoculars for personal and military use and brought back many memories to me from years in the past. However, more importantly was the people aspect and the stories they had with binoculars that was very interesting and I think this is the first time this has been done. In any event, it pushed me to do something with a book on optics including binoculars to educate and inform consumers about what they can do with sport optics and surely many of them will have their own stories to tell about their instruments use in various ways.

I want to thank many of the people who have made this book possible. Unfortunately, there are too many to list all of them here and thus I will generalize several categories:

- I want to thank all of the companies who supplied images of their products that I have included in this book.

- I want to thank the various people who read the manuscript and had the expertise in their particular field to help me. They read the document, reviewed, offered suggestions and helped immensely to make sure the book would be as accurate as possible. Of course, some areas are subjective and some minor disagreements were unavoidable but I appreciate other points of view.

- I want to thank a number of friends who edited various parts of the book, helped me with making the charts, helped edit changes to images and other aspects to finish the book. An extra thanks to Josh Lazenby for doing a complete edit.

- I want to give a special thanks to Cherie, my wife, who had to put up with long nights and weekends by me in writing the book.

Table of Contents

Preface 10

Chapter 1 How to Choose Sport Optics 12

Chapter 2 Where Can You Purchase Sport Optics? 16

    Brands sold in the U.S.A. 17

Chapter 3 What is a Binocular, Spotting Scope, or Riflescope? 19

    What is a Binocular? 19

    What is a Spotting Scope? 26

    What is a Riflescope? 31

Chapter 4 What can a Binocular and Spotting Scope be used for? ... 37

Chapter 5 Can a Particular Size Be Best for a Hobby? 40

Chapter 6 Special Sport Optics 42

    Specialized Binoculars 42

    Specialized Spotting Scopes 46

    Specialized Riflescopes 47

Chapter 7 How to Expand Your Usage of Sport Optics 49

    Birding 49

    Astronomy 52

    Target Shooting 55

Chapter 8 Criteria in Choosing Sport Optics 57

    Metric Conversion 57

Chapter 9 Optics Details 58

    Optical Systems 58

    Power (Magnification) 62

    Objective Lenses 69

    Eyepieces 72

    Prisms 73

    Field Lenses 77

    Focus Lenses 77

    Erecting Lenses 77

    Optical Coatings 78

Field of View..83

Eye Relief..85

Near (Close) Focus 87

Depth of Field...88

Exit Pupil..89

Brightness...92

Light Transmission 94

Resolution (Resolving Power) 95

Contrast...98

Chapter 10   Optical Aberrations 99

Collimation (Alignment) 102

Chapter 11   Controls for Sport Optics Products...104

Adjustment Controls for Binoculars..104

Adjustment Controls for Spotting Scopes..108

Adjustment Controls for Riflescopes 111

Chapter 12   Riflescope Details 115

Riflescope Tubes 115

Reticles 119

Parallax...130

Chapter 13 More Factors to Consider for Sport Optics 132

Waterproof Optical Products...132

Warranty 134

Chapter 14   Final Items for Decision Making 135

Binoculars..135

Spotting Scopes...140

Riflescopes 144

Chapter 15   Inspection, Storing, Cleaning and Repair 149

Initial Inspection..149

Storing and Caring for Optical Products 150

Cleaning Optical Surfaces..151

Repair 152

Chapter 16   Who Manufactures Optical Products? 153

Chapter 17   What New Technology Will Be Coming? 155

Appendix A   Metric and English Conversion 156

Appendix B   Exit Pupil (EP) Size of Optical Instruments 157

Appendix C   Relative Brightness Index (RBI) 159

Appendix D   Twilight Factor (TF) 161

Appendix E   Mil-Dot Range Guide – Distance in Yards 163

Appendix F   Mil-Dot Range Guide – Distance in Meters 164

Appendix G   Books on Birding 165

Appendix H   Books on Astronomy using Binoculars 167

Appendix I   Books on Optics for Hunting 169

Appendix J   Books on Target Shooting 171

Appendix K   Binoculars – U.S.A. Imports 173

Appendix L   Riflescopes – U.S.A. Imports 177

Summary 181

About the Author 182

Courtesy of Minox

Courtesy of Swarovski

Courtesy of Tony Hallas/astrophoto.com

Mircea Bezergheanu/Shutterstock

Courtesy of Carl Zeiss

Courtesy of Zeiss

Preface

Why write a book on binoculars, spotting scopes, and riflescopes? You might think that they are something that you pick up, aim and look through. Well, there is more to it than that.

Being in the optical business for over fifty years, I have gained an appreciation for good optical instruments. Binoculars, spotting scopes, and riflescopes vary considerably in quality — there are excellent ones, very good ones, good ones, satisfactory ones, and very poor ones.

8.5x42

Courtesy of Swarovski

Depending on what you will use the optics for, there are certain specifications you should know. Unfortunately, many manufacturers do not tell you all the specifications (some do not want you to know) that may be important but they do give you a lot of marketing hype and pretty pictures.

You might think that you can go online, to the library, or bookstore and learn about binoculars, spotting scopes, and riflescopes, as I tried. However, it is amazing that there are few books on the subject of optics. True, there are many magazine articles periodically on optics but only a few that are well written and factual but the majority have subject matter too short and many times with erroneous or misleading information.

Thus, I want to give you, the consumer, as much information as possible, giving you honest facts that will help give you a better understanding of optics.

Binoculars are used for so many applications with the largest category being for hunting, then for bird watching, then for sporting event usage, and then for astronomy. Spotting scope usage is extensive for hunting and birding as well as wildlife viewing and astronomy. Riflescopes are useful for sport hunting and target shooting.

2.5-10x42

Courtesy of Leica

Hunting is a huge category in the U.S.A. with a rich tradition since the beginning of the country. Hunting is also a large category in many other countries around the world with a long history dated back centuries. It provides an outdoor experience like no other. Hunting comes with a requirement, to understand and intimately know the land and the game. Hunters for the most part are passionate about their sport. Hunters are also very ardent conservationists and environmentalists who wish to protect our land.

Bird watchers are also very passionate about their hobby and are ardent conservationists and environmentalists, who want to see our land preserved and protected as well.

Writing this book presented a great challenge to discuss both bird watching and sport hunting but it is very interesting to note that many hunters are bird watchers and vice versa. They all use optics and that is the main emphasis of this book.

I appreciate optics especially excellent ones and how they can enhance whatever outdoor interests you have.

20-60x85

Courtesy of Zeiss

I am by no means an expert in optics. However, I have learned a lot of invaluable information over the years from being in the optical industry and extensively using optical instruments. When I have needed outside advice on optics, I have contacted optics professionals.

Therefore, in an effort to share with you the basics of standard optical binoculars, spotting scopes, and riflescopes for whatever you use them for as well as who offers them and what the specifications are, this book is to help you. I would be pleased if any information in this book helps anyone make a better purchasing decision.

I say "optical" products and most of the detailed discussion concerns the standard type products. If I had discussed specialty type optical products in detail, it would have required a much larger book and I would never have finished it.

Optical products are required in many military and law enforcement activities. However, this book is primarily for consumers.

Chapter 1   How to Choose Sport Optics

It is very easy to choose a binocular, spotting scope, or riflescope for many people. They think that a binocular is an instrument you pick up and just look through – simple and easy. They may buy a pretty-looking spotting scope with high magnification and a low price, then mount it on a tripod and they think they are ready to use it and all will be good. They think a riflescope is this black tube with glass installed at each end. So, all they have to do is select a low price, fancy model name along with an attractive color and style. If people do this, in most cases they will be disappointed.

What else is important? What you are going to do and how are you going to use the binocular, spotting scope, or riflescope, and how serious you want to become in your interests will help determine the best product for you.

8x42

Courtesy of Nikon

My recommendation is to buy the most expensive optical instrument that you can afford (after you have decided on the type you want) and you will not be sorry! Optics, with proper care, should last many years and the upfront purchasing investment will be well worth it.

For hunters it may make sense to spend more on a riflescope than the rifle as the riflescope is so important in getting an accurate shot – you know the rifle will shoot fine but if you cannot aim it properly to get a precise shot all is for naught.

Binoculars and spotting scopes appear to be simple optical devices but in reality, they are complex, precision optical instruments.

Riflescopes are even more complex as they have to function with heavy recoil action of the rifle and stand up to this hundreds of times and yet continue to be repeatedly accurate.

Courtesy of Celestron
20-60x80

An educated consumer will be much happier learning about the various aspects of binoculars, spotting scopes, and riflescopes before making a purchase.

This book discusses the basics of sport optics products and gives you a lot of information to digest. It should help you make the best choice considering what you will be using the products for before making your buying decision.

In general, with binoculars, spotting scopes, and riflescopes you usually get what you pay for. As the price increases, in most cases, so does the quality of the unit. It is easier to use

2-12x42

Image Courtesy of Leupold & Stevens, Inc.

this guideline for binoculars and spotting scopes because with riflescopes there are so many different types of options to skew the pricing. However, this is just a guideline as I have seen and compared several products costing a few hundred dollars outperform models costing two to four times as much.

Be very careful with television, online, and print ads for binoculars that offer you 1000 power, see sharply at 35 miles, and many other deceptive and irrelevant claims, many free extras, and all at a price of $19.98 plus shipping and handling.

I've seen a TV ad for "Zoomies" that magnify 300 times and the optics are put into an eyeglass like frame, noting great for reading books, TV watching, binocular use, etc. – and all for $10 plus shipping and handling and get a second one free with order.

Do not fall for binoculars (large or small aperture) with powers of 120x, 150x or more as the image will last brightness, have a very narrow field and not satisfactory at all.

There are many more similar type horrible products but just ignore them as you will be throwing your money away as they are junk. Stick with known, reputable brands.

There is a multitude of binoculars, spotting scopes, and riflescopes available in the marketplace in the U.S.A. from dozens of manufacturers and suppliers and when added to what is available in other countries around the world it is mind-boggling. It can be very confusing trying to sort through the maze. Most brands are reputable but be careful of unknown brands.

To give you an idea of how many models are available at this time in the U.S.A. alone, I tallied the numbers by looking at company brochures and on their websites, by going to numerous conventions and events, etc. If I were to add brands sold exclusively in Europe and other countries around the world, I am sure the models would be increased about 30% to 50%. These are standard optical models and not including specialized binoculars, spotting scopes, or riflescopes. The retail price range for these instruments is below. Due to the large quantity of the various products, I have included images throughout the book of many of the more popular models.

Binoculars   *– over 2,000 models*

Retail pricing (MAP or Street) from $7.99 to $2799.00

10x42

Courtesy of Kenko

Spotting Scopes   *– over 400 models*

Retail pricing (MAP or Street) from $24.99 to $3899.00

20-60x70

Courtesy of Konus

Riflescopes   *– over 3,000 models*

Retail pricing (MAP or Street) from $9.99 to $3729.00

4.5-30x50

Courtesy of Bushnell

I cannot tell you which particular binocular, spotting scope, or riflescope is best for your application as *only you can choose* the unit best suited for your particular purpose and usage. This book can be a guide to help you make your choice or choices as you may want two or more binoculars or riflescopes for different applications.

It is amazing that in some manufacturers' brochures and websites for binoculars you are told that model "X" is the best for birding, model "Y" is the best for sporting events, model "Z" is best for hunting, etc. Then, they will tell you which riflescope to buy for specific hunting categories. To me this is ridiculous because it depends on exactly what you are going to be doing, under what conditions, and what your budget is.

It also does not help you that many retail store clerks know virtually nothing about the optical instruments they are selling. There are many specialty retail shops and online business (especially in the hunting and birding industries) where the personnel are quite knowledgeable. So, read on and hopefully you will gain some knowledge about binoculars, spotting scopes, and riflescopes.

4.5-14x42

Courtesy of Burris

20-60x85

Courtesy of Vortex Optics

10x42

Courtesy of Vortex Optics

Chapter 2 Where Can You Purchase Sport Optics?

As noted earlier, there are over 2,000 models of binoculars, over 3,000 models of riflescopes and over 400 models of spotting scopes in the U.S.A. let alone another huge number if including brands specific to other parts of the world. Retail pricing runs from under ten dollars to several thousands of dollars.

There are presently 50 brands of spotting scopes, 63 brands of riflescopes, and 69 brands of binoculars.

Thus, the choice to buy would seem overwhelming and it can be. I hope that information provided in this book can make your shopping experience easier and not so stressful.

Once you are ready to shop, there are numerous places to make purchases:

- Sporting Goods stores
- Online Specialty Optics retailers
- Birding specialty shops
- Nature Centers/shops
- Gun Shops
- Museum stores
- Birding festivals/events
- Amazon
- Outdoor Equipment suppliers
- Specialty Mail Order Catalogs
- Astronomy specialty shops
- Electronic stores
- Websites of some brands
- Photographic specialty shops
- Department stores

The above list is only some of the retailers offering sport optics and many others offer these products. Some of the retailers have very experienced staff to answer any questions you may have about products.

The vast number of competitive brands in the marketplace alone is staggering. However, do your research. Following this section, I list the brands offering various sport optics products. I encourage you to browse information at various websites.

Brands sold in the U.S.A.
Optical Binoculars (B), Riflescopes (R), and Spotting Scopes (S)

Brand	Website	R	B	S
Aim Sports	www.aimsportsinc.com	X		
Alpen Outdoor	www.alpenoptics.com	X	X	X
ATN	www.atncorp.com		X	
Barska	www.barska.com	X	X	X
Bass Pro Shops	www.basspro.com	X	X	X
(Oculus/Pursuit house brands)				
Bresser USA	www.bresser.com	X	X	X
Browe	www.browe-inc.com	X		
Brunton	www.brunton.com	X	X	X
BSA Optics	www.bsaoptics.com	X	X	X
Burris	www.burrisoptics.com	X		X
Bushnell	www.bushnell.com	X	X	X
Cabela's (Euro/Alaskan/Powderhorn/	www.cabelas.com	X	X	X
Slugger house brands)				
Canon	www.usa.canon.com		X	
Carson Optical	www.carson.com	X	X	X
Celestron	www.celestron.com		X	X
Centerpoint	www.crosman.com	X	X	
Clearidge Optics	www.clearidgeoptics.com	X		
Counter Sniper	www.countersniperoptics.com	X		
Cstar	n/a		X	
Crosman	www.crosman.com	X		
Dick's Sporting Goods	www.dickssportinggoods.com	X	X	X
(Field & Stream house brand)				
Docter Optics	www.browe-inc.com	X	X	
Eagle Optics + Atlas Optics house brand	www.eagleoptics.com		X	
Emerson	n/a		X	
Eschenbach Optik	www.eschenbach.com		X	
Falcon Optics	www.falconoptics.com	X		
Firefield	www.fire-field.com	X	X	X
Gamo	www.gamousa.com	X		
Garrett Optical	www.garrettoptical.com		X	
Hawke Sport Optics	www.hawkeoptics.com	X	X	X
Horus Vision	www.horusvision.com	X		
Kahles	www.kahles.at	X	X	
Kenko	www.kenkoglobal.com		X	X
Konus U.S.A.	www.konus.com	X	X	X
Kowa	www.kowasporting.com		X	X
Kruger Optical	www.krugeroptical.com	X	X	X
Laxco	www.laxcoinc.com		X	
Leapers	www.leapers.com	X		
Leatherwood/Hi-Lux	www.hi-luxoptics.com	X		
Leica	www.leica-camera.com	X	X	X
Leupold & Stevens	www.leupold.com	X	X	X
Meade Instruments	www.meade.com		X	X
Meopta USA	www.meoptasportsoptics.com	X	X	X
Millett	www.millettsights.com	X		

Brands	Website	R	B	S
Minox	www.minox.com	X	X	X
Mueller Optics	www.muelleroptics.com	X		
National Geographic	www.bresser.com		X	X
NcStar	www.ncstar.com	X	X	X
Newcon	www.newcon-optik.com		X	X
Nightforce	www.nightforceoptics.com	X		
Nikko Stirling	www.nikkostirling.com	X	X	
Nikon	www.nikonhunting.com	X	X	X
Oberwerk	www.oberwerk.com		X	
Olivon	www.olivonmanufacturing.com	X	X	X
Olympus	www.getolympus.com		X	
Opticron	www.opticronusa.com		X	X
Optolyth	www.valdada.com		X	X
Orion Telescope	www.telescope.com		X	X
Osprey Worldwide	www.miniosprey.com	X		
Pentax Imaging	www.pentaximaging.com	X	X	X
Premier Reticles	www.premierreticles.com	X		
Pride Fowler	www.rapidreticle.com	X		
ProMariner	www.pmariner.com		X	
Pulsar	www.pulsarnightvisionusa.com		X	
Redfield	www.redfield.com	X	X	X
Rokinon	www.rokinon.com		X	X
Schmidt & Bender	www.schmidtandbender.com	X		
Selsi	www.techopticsinternational.com		X	
Shepherd	www.shepherdscopes.com	X	X	
Sightmark	www.sightmark.com	X	X	X
Sightron	www.sightron.com	X	X	X
Simmons	www.simmonsoptics.com	X	X	X
Steiner	www.steiner-binoculars.com	X	X	
Sun Optics USA	www.sunopticsusa.com	X	X	X
Swarovski	www.swarovskioptik.com	X	X	X
Swift Sport Optics	www.swift-sportoptics.com	X	X	X
Tasco	www.tasco.com	X	X	X
Tele Vue Optics	www.televue.com			X
Thompson/Center	www.tcarms.com	X		
Traditions	www.traditionsfirearms.com	X		
Trijicon	www.trijicon.com	X		
TruGlo	www.truglo.com	X	X	
US Optics	www.usoptics.com	X		
Valdada IOR Optics	www.valdada.com	X	X	
Vanguard	www.vanguardworld.com		X	X
Vivitar	www.vivitar.com		X	X
Vixen Sport Optics	www.vixensportoptics.com	X	X	X
Vortex Optics	www.vortexoptics.com	X	X	X
Weaver	www.weaveroptics.com	X	X	X
William Optics	www.williamoptics.com		X	
Yukon Optics	www.yukonopticsglobal.com			X
Zeiss, Carl	www.zeiss.com/hunting	X	X	X
Zen Ray Optics	www.zen-ray.com		X	X
Zhumell	www.zhumell.com		X	X

Chapter 3   What is a Binocular, Spotting Scope, or Riflescope?

What is a Binocular?

Simply, a binocular is two low-powered astronomical telescopes mounted together. As compared to a spotting scope, binoculars allow you a more comfortable viewing experience by using both eyes in a relaxed manner with a three-dimensional view.

Any binocular has two basic functions:

1.   To gather more light than the unaided human eye does
2.   To enlarge the image of what you are looking at

However, a binocular is much more than a basic definition. A binocular can:

- Open up new vistas of learning
- Add pleasure to your life
- Create excitement with new discoveries
- Help while hunting when searching terrain for game
- Add new dimensions to whatever you enjoy looking at
- Expand hobbies to gain more fulfillment
- Aid in your appreciation of the world
- Allow families or friends to share the enjoyment of observing

Courtesy of Swarovski

Do not be embarrassed to ask questions about products that you may have or are interested in and remember that no question is stupid as it is important to you. With binoculars, two questions commonly asked quite often:

- How far can I see?
- What is the most power (magnification is a frequently used synonym) I can get?

Both questions are quite valid and they are the same ones that I asked when first introduced to optical products and being quite naive.

Our naked eye allows us to see the Moon that is an average 238,900 miles (384,500 kilometers) away. We can see Saturn which is 800 million miles (1.29 billion kilometers) away, we can look at deep sky objects like the Andromeda Galaxy which is the nearest galaxy to ours and it is 2.5 million light years away (a light year is 6 trillion miles or 10 trillion kilometers). However, to see objects on our own Earth, there are limits to what details we can see by the atmosphere with its varying environmental conditions. Thus, the limits to what optical instruments can actually see mean you need to consider carefully the optical quality and specifications of the products.

Courtesy of Leica   10x42

Power is arrived by the optical design and higher powers are not always the best choice.

Binoculars come in a multitude of sizes and powers but the majority range in power from 7x to 10x with objective lens sizes of 25mm to 50mm.

Giant binoculars are those with objective lens sizes of 70mm and larger and these typically are used mounted on rigid tripods. These large binoculars are for astronomy **and** for terrestrial applications.

The choice of prism type has a large effect on the physical size of binoculars. Roof prisms are in-line designs so they are longer and narrower while Porro prisms types are shorter and wider. This is confirmed in the images that follow.

Roof Prism Binoculars – Full Size

8x42

Image Courtesy of Leupold & Stevens, Inc.

8x32

Courtesy of Nikon

Courtesy of Steiner

10x56

8x42

Courtesy of Celestron

10x42

10x43

Courtesy of Pentax

Courtesy of Konus

Roof Prism Binoculars – Full Size

10x42

Courtesy of Vortex Optics

10x42

Courtesy of Bushnell

10x42

Courtesy of Alpen

8x42

Courtesy of Zeiss

8x42

Courtesy of Vanguard

Courtesy of Minox   **10x43**

Roof Prism Binoculars – Compact Size

8x25

Courtesy of Nikon

10x32

Courtesy of Sightron

8x26

Courtesy of Carson Optical

10x25   **Courtesy of Bushnell**

Courtesy of Vanguard   **10x25**

10x25   Courtesy of Celestron

Porro Prism Binoculars – Full and Compact Sizes

8x42

Courtesy of Nikon

10x50

Courtesy of Bushnell

8x40

Courtesy of Celestron

Courtesy of Pentax

8x40

7x26

Courtesy of Bushnell

8x25

Courtesy of Nikon

Giant Binoculars

25x100

Courtesy of Celestron

20/40x100

Courtesy of Barska

12-60x70

Courtesy of Barska

25/40x100

Courtesy of Oberwerk

25/40x100

Courtesy of Oberwerk

15x70

Courtesy of Celestron

What is a Spotting Scope?

Simply, a spotting scope is a small refractor or catadioptric astronomical telescope. The spotting scope mounts to a photographic/video tripod for stability while using it.

Any spotting scope has two basic functions:

1. To gather more light than the unaided human eye does
2. To enlarge the image of what you're looking at, normally at long distances

However, a spotting scope is much more than a basic definition. A spotting scope can:

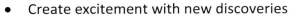

- Open up new vistas of learning and pleasure to your life
- Create excitement with new discoveries
- Help while hunting when searching terrain for game at long distances
- Convenience for target shooting to evaluate your results on the targets
- Add new dimensions to whatever you enjoy looking at
- Expand hobbies to gain more fulfillment like birding, hunting, wildlife observation and astronomy
- Aid in your appreciation of the world

Spotting scopes come in a variety of magnifications by using eyepieces. Some are of fixed power and most of these are in a range from 12x up to 30x. Others have interchangeable eyepieces with different powers (10x up to 60x normally), and others are variable (zoom) models which are by far the most popular (ranges from 12 to 40x, 15 to 45x, and 20 to 60x, and other powers). The variable models are quick to go from low to high power or anywhere in between.

20-60x85

Courtesy of Vortex Optics

Typical objective lens sizes range from 30mm to 100mm or larger and you will find numerous models of varying sizes and magnification ranges. The most popular models are with 60mm and 80mm objective lenses.

Lower powers will give you the brightest images with the widest field of view. This is great in scanning distant objects. Higher powers will allow you to see more details. For example, when hunting you can see details at low powers that you cannot see with binoculars and you can see hidden game, and see further details at higher powers.

Spotting scopes come mainly in one of two styles – straight through (where you look straight through the eyepiece in a straight line) and in an angled view (where you look at the object at an angle of 45°). The choice between the two is a personal one determined by what type of viewing you will be doing and many other factors. The angled types are the most popular and are fine for finding objects after you get used to the spotting scope. The angled

13-30x50

Courtesy of Nikon

scopes are easier to use when two or more people are sharing the spotting scope on a tripod rather than having a pain in your neck or constantly changing the tripod height.

Most spotting scopes are adaptable for taking images (snapshots or video) with the proper adapters – called digiscoping. There are various adapters required depending on your particular spotting scope to use point and shoot digital cameras, SLR cameras, and DSLR cameras. Some digital spotting scopes have built-in cameras.

There are hybrids to what most people think are spotting scopes. Tele Vue turns astronomical systems into excellent refractor spotting scopes and Celestron offers very good Maksutov and Schmidt-Cassegrain spotting scopes all of which look different.

Courtesy of Zeiss

Spotting Scopes

20-70x82

Courtesy of Meopta

16-48x65

Courtesy of Vortex Optics

20-60x82

Courtesy of Vanguard

20-60x65

Courtesy of Pentax

20-60x80

Courtesy of Celestron

13-30x50

Courtesy of Nikon

Spotting Scopes

20-75x85

Courtesy of Zeiss

20-60x88

Courtesy of Kowa

15-45x65

Courtesy of Barska

20-60x80

Courtesy of Alpen

18-36x50

Courtesy of Kenko

20-60x80

Courtesy of Sightron

Spotting Scopes

25-75x82

Courtesy of Nikon

20-60x85

Courtesy of Sightron

18-36x60

Courtesy of Alpen

15-45x65

Courtesy of Vortex Optics

30x85

Courtesy of Tele Vue

39x90

Courtesy of Celestron

What is a Riflescope?

Objective Bell   Elevation Adjustment   Windage Adjustment   Eyepiece

Objective Lens   Adjustable Objective Side Focus   Zoom Ring   Ocular Lens

Courtesy of Bushnell

Simply, a riflescope is similar to a refractor astronomical telescope. These are magnified optical instruments for purposes of this book. There are specialty types of riflescopes included as well.

Any riflescope has three basic functions:

1. To gather more light than the unaided human eye does
2. To enlarge the image of what you're looking at
3. To aim at a target and ensure an accurate shot mounted on a rifle.

Riflescopes are for hunting and target shooting. They are telescopic sights. Many in the hunting industry call riflescopes "scopes" which can be confusing to some people. Some people call spotting scopes "telescopes", etc. Therefore, definitions in this book are:

A. Riflescope – the term is used for scopes attached to rifles
B. Spotting Scope – the term is used for terrestrial spotting scopes for various observations usually at long distances
C. Telescope – the term is used for astronomical telescopes used for looking up in the sky

5-20x50

Courtesy of Trijicon

Riflescopes are for hunting as well as for target shooting.

Some hunters attempt to use their riflescopes to glass where glassing is a term meaning searching terrain for game. This is dangerous! A hunter should not point his rifle at anything he does not intend to shoot! Binoculars are used to glass for game and are the best choice for this as you are using both eyes to reduce eyestrain and fatigue. More importantly, you will see the game before it sees you and you can then carefully aim your riflescope in time to get off a precision shot. The bottom line – binoculars are designed and intended for long-range viewing (looking for game) and riflescopes are designed and intended for aiming which allows you to clearly see the target and take an accurate shot.

Riflescopes have been around since the 1860s. Not until the late 1940s did manufacturers continue to make improvements that offered hunters reliable products. Then, riflescopes started their rise in replacing traditional iron sights. Since the 1960s few revolutionary changes have been made but more precision manufacturing and changes to state-of-the-art materials used (metals, glass, coatings, reticles, etc.) have made them sturdier, more consistent, and more accurate.

A riflescope magnifies your target so you can easily see it compared to the naked eye. This allows you to shoot more precisely at long distances and increases the safety factor as you can see the target clearly (versus guessing) and what lies in front and behind the target.

A riflescope allows for more hunting time (dawn and dusk) since you have increased light gathering ability. Viewing an animal at 9x, 6x, or even 2x shows so much more detail than your naked eye.

1-5x23

Courtesy of Weaver

Reticles within the riflescope allow for precise and accurate shots. For a riflescope to perform properly, it must be "mounted" properly to the rifle and be "sighted-in" accurately.

Riflescopes

3-12x56

Courtesy of Zeiss

2-12x42

Image Courtesy of Leupold & Stevens, Inc.

4.5-14x42

Courtesy of Burris

6-24x42

Courtesy of Weaver

2.5-10x42

3-15x50

Courtesy of Minox

Courtesy of Steiner

Riflescopes

6-24x50

Courtesy of Vortex Optics

2-8x32

Courtesy of Nikon

3-9x40

Courtesy of Bushnell

2.5-10x32

Courtesy of Nightforce

4.5-14x44

Courtesy of Carson Optical

8.5-32x52

Courtesy of Konus

Riflescopes

3-9x40

Courtesy of Pentax

10x42

Courtesy of Sightron

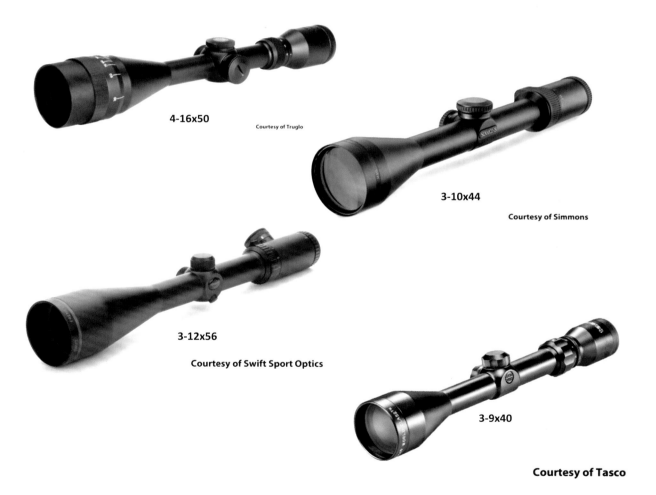

4-16x50

Courtesy of Truglo

3-10x44

Courtesy of Simmons

3-12x56

Courtesy of Swift Sport Optics

3-9x40

Courtesy of Tasco

Riflescopes

3-12x56

Courtesy of Meopta

4-12x40

Courtesy of Alpen

10-40x50

Courtesy of Barska

3-12x50

Courtesy of Trijicon

2.5-10x42

Courtesy of Leica

3-12x50

Courtesy of Swarovski

Courtesy of Redfield

2-7x34

Chapter 4   What can a Binocular and Spotting Scope be used for?

Courtesy of Pentax

Courtesy of Simmons

Using a binocular or a spotting scope is to look at virtually anything that you look at with your eyes and greatly enhance that view. Possible applications include:

- Astronomy
- Backpacking
- Birding
- Boating (binoculars only)
- Camping
- Concerts (binoculars only)
- Fishing
- Flying (binoculars only)
- Government – law enforcement/military, air traffic control, search & rescue, security, and many other facets of local, state, and federal agencies
- Hiking
- Hunting
- Long Distance Observations
- Museum Visits (binoculars only)
- Nature Study
- Sporting Events
- Surveillance
- Target Shooting
- Theater/Opera (binoculars only)
- Travel
- View Home Applications

Courtesy of Tasco

DECEMBER 27th, 2012
03:44:18 UTC (20 mins)
N
L P

Courtesy of Damian Peach

Eq Diam 16.0" Alt: 34°   D. Peach

Courtesy of Tasco

38

Courtesy of Tasco

Courtesy of Bushnell

Courtesy of Tony Hallas/astrophoto.com

Chapter 5   Can a Particular Size Be Best for a Hobby?

As I mentioned earlier, it depends on the circumstances. I will give you a few examples of the wide range of uses. To understand the numbers below, the first one like "8" is the power or "1-4" is the zoom power range and the second one like "21" is the objective lens diameter in millimeters.

For birding, an 8x21 binocular may be just fine on a bright day for observing a hummingbird at your bird feeder 15 feet (460cm) away. Most birding is done with an 8x42 or 10x42 or sizes close to this which is good in bright conditions but essential in low light (dawn or dusk or on cloudy days). However, if you are observing an eagle's nest 1/2 mile (0.8km) away, this may call for a 15x70 or 20x80 model on a tripod. If you are out on a field trip in a dark forest, you may need a pair of 10x42, 8x56 or 10x50 binoculars.

Courtesy of Kowa

If you are in a large arena watching a soccer match or football game, it depends on your seat location (are you at midfield in the first few rows or are you behind the goals at the top of the stadium?). A 7x35 binocular might be your choice for midfield, and a 10x50 for behind goals up high. It also depends on whether the game is a day or a night game. The night game is better with larger objective lenses.

Courtesy of Damian Peach

For astronomy, a pair of 7x35 binoculars may be fine for observing the Moon or wide star fields. A 10x50 binocular will get you started to find deep sky objects such as galaxies, nebulae, star clusters and allows you to split many double stars. However, to observe details of the Moon and to see more detail on planets, you need higher power and larger objective lenses.

For observing many deep sky objects, you need large aperture (70mm up to 150mm) binoculars mounted on a very sturdy tripod or other rigid platform.

For the mariner, most manufacturers say that 7x50 is the ideal size. This is a good low light performing binocular but if great distances are what you are after, then a 10x50 might be better.

For hunting, an 8x42 binocular may be best for close distances in a thick forest but a 10x56 or 15x56 may be better over wide expanses of prairie, desert, or mountains.

Courtesy of Bushnell

12-36x60

Courtesy of Celestron

For birding, binoculars are the first thing you use. However, for long distances you may need the extra magnification of a 20-60x80 spotting scope to see fine details. If you are hiking long distances up hills, the views may dictate to use a spotting scope but the weight may make you reconsider this.

Courtesy of Tasco

For hunting, a 1-4x24 may be all you need for big and dangerous game. If you hunt for small varmints or prairie dogs at long distances, you may want a 4-16x32. If you mainly hunt for deer, a 3-9x40 may be appropriate.

So, you can see from these brief examples that the size binocular, spotting scope, or riflescope you choose depends on the circumstances. In many cases, you will find that a single pair of binoculars or a single riflescope is not enough and you may eventually want two, three or more different instruments for various applications.

Chapter 6   Special Sport Optics

There are optical products available that have specialized functions.

Specialized Binoculars

Monoculars

A monocular is half of a binocular. It is much lighter and more compact than a binocular. Many brands offer at least one monocular as part of their offerings.

8x25

Courtesy of Vortex Optics

Prior to the last decade, most monoculars all looked the same (just a straight tube without any style to them) and were mainly 8x21 or 10x25. Currently there are a lot of different cosmetic styles to choose from and a variety of powers and aperture.

The general range of powers is from 5x up to 12x and a few are below or above these powers. There are now models that are zoom monoculars.

Monoculars are very useful for the same applications as binoculars and should be considered for their versatility and portability especially for hiking, hunting, birding, backpacking and other activities where weight is important. Having a monocular in your car, purse, pocket, or backpack allows you to have optics available at a moment's notice when sudden unexpected opportunities arise.

5x15

Courtesy of Nikon   I consider a usable monocular to be in the range of 15 to 42mm for the objective lenses. Smaller than 15mm is just too small to be very useful. Monoculars over 42mm in diameter are considered being a spotting scope.

Like binoculars, many monoculars are available as waterproof. Monoculars generally have a near focus in the range of 10 to 20 feet (305 to 610cm). But, some units focus as close as one foot (30cm).

Courtesy of Celestron

There are even specialized units offered to aid golfers in their game. These have a built-in distance scale to determine the distance to the pin.

Several monoculars have reticles installed for distance measurements and others have compasses installed for directional information.

Opera Glasses

Opera glasses (a form of binoculars) are low power, compact optical instruments. These are simple, compact devices utilizing only lenses with no need for erecting prisms. Several decades in the past, full size Galilean binoculars (called field glasses) were quite common for their simplicity. Advances in Porro prism and roof prism optical designs have eliminated the need for full size Galilean types.

Courtesy of Celestron

Opera glasses have a typical magnification range of 2x to 5x. Objective lens sizes range from 12 to 30mm, which is good for concerts, operas, theater, indoor sporting events, or any event where you need some magnification to see the stage, field or other facility where conventional binoculars are too powerful for many situations. Higher magnifications with a wide field of view are not possible with opera glasses.

They are rugged, lightweight, and small. They are good for children as they are more durable since they lack a prism assembly that could come out of alignment. However, the optical quality is not as good as most prism type binoculars and they do not have an adjustment to correct for the vision difference between a person's left and right eye as discussed later in the book.

Very few manufacturers offer opera glasses, which is a shame since they are very useful.

Image Stabilized Binoculars

Image stabilized binoculars are binoculars which have a means for reducing or eliminating the motion or movement of the view seen when looking through them. The motion or vibration of the image comes from the unsteadiness of our arms and hands or from a moving vehicle. They allow you to see fainter objects

Courtesy of Nikon

and bring out much more detail that you ever thought possible as compared to similar size non-stabilized binoculars unless they were placed on a sturdy tripod.

Canon

I have used various models from all the manufacturers. The views seen are so enjoyable and they are very comfortable to use. As an example, I have observed a red-tailed hawk nest about 400 yards (366 meters) away while handholding the image stabilized binoculars and watched the young nestlings go through their early life cycle – this would not have been possible with standard binoculars unless mounted on a tripod.

There are passive designs where the stabilization is controlled by gyroscopes. Then there are active designs using sensors. The sensors are part of the binocular, either prisms or lenses, and controlled to correct the binocular shaking or movement.

There are also some mechanical designs but the movement continues for such a long time on the ones I tried that they were not satisfactory at all. So, stay with digital types.

The steady image is quite enjoyable especially when holding the binocular for any length of time. Bird watchers, hunters, nature observers, astronomers, mariners and people viewing distant scenery can all benefit from using these.

A few companies (Nikon, Zeiss, Fujinon, and Canon to name a few) are offering these binoculars and they are expensive but the benefits may outweigh the cost and heavy weight.

Night Vision Monoculars and Binoculars

Night vision optics have the ability to see in low light conditions and in total darkness.

There are mainly two types of these binoculars:

Courtesy of Bushnell

A. Intensity range – image enhancement is by using an image intensifier tube or other means. The image is a green color and they have been around for many years but are not a large factor any longer. They detect small amounts of visible light (even from stars) and amplify it so we can see an image.

   Newer digital technology has a built-in infrared illuminator to allow usage in ambient light or in total darkness. The images are clearer, brighter and sharper.

B. Spectral range – thermal images from the enhanced spectral range obtained using near infrared or ultraviolet radiation. When first introduced only black and white images were possible. During the last decade, digital color models became available. This type of technology does not detect any light but it does collect the infrared radiation from bodies (human or animal) and other warm objects to form an image.

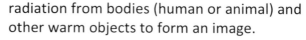

There are many uses for night vision binoculars – pilots, farmers, boaters, hikers, hunters, astronomers, military, and law enforcement to name a few. A few of the popular brands are ATN, Bushnell, Carson Optical, Newcon, Pulsar, Sightmark, and Yukon.

Courtesy of Carson Optical

GPS Binoculars

GPS binoculars have been around for a number of years but not very many of them are available. They are very useful for giving you GPS coordinates. Newer versions have a built-in LCD along with a digital compass to be able to see the information easily. Some models give the user elevation and other information.

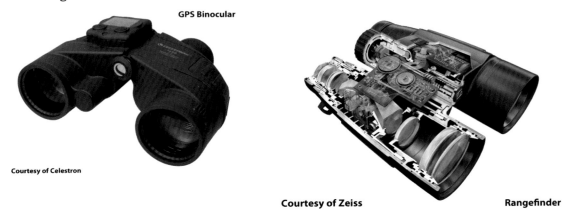

GPS Binocular

Courtesy of Celestron

Courtesy of Zeiss   Rangefinder

Binocular Rangefinders

Binocular rangefinders are compact and handy electronic devices to use for determining distances up to 1000 yards (meters) and more on some models. The common rangefinders available are laser rangefinders from Bushnell, Leica, Swarovski, and Zeiss.

Rangefinders make distances easier to determine by hunters, mariners and hikers. The military and law enforcement and other agencies have many uses for these products.

Digital Binoculars

Digital binoculars are a combination binocular and built-in digital camera. You can take snapshot images or video and the captured image is the same magnification seen in the binocular on many models.

Courtesy of Bushnell

There are many different features depending on the brand and model. Many have optical zoom as well as a digital zoom to increase the power but the digital zoom results may not be so good.

Digital binoculars were a big fad during the 2000s with many different brands and many models available but today they have virtually disappeared from the market due to their low resolution, smart phones with cameras and point and shoot cameras with increasing resolution and lower costs. Bushnell and Barska are two of the main suppliers now.

Specialized Spotting Scopes

Digital Spotting Scopes

Digital spotting scopes are a combination spotting scope with a built-in digital camera. You can take snapshot images or video and the captured image is at the same magnification as seen through the spotting scope on most models.

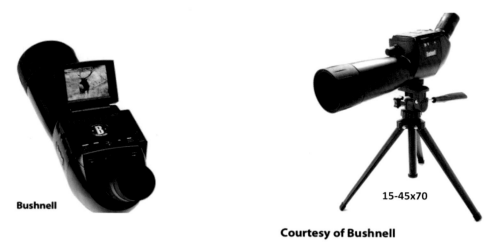

Bushnell

15-45x70

Courtesy of Bushnell

There are many different features depending on the brand and model. Many have optical zoom as well as a digital zoom to increase the power.

It is an easy way to take images when carrying and using your spotting scope and you do not want to bring your camera along.

Digital spotting scopes were a fad during the 2000s with several brands and a large number of models available but today they have virtually disappeared from the market due to their low resolution, smart phones with high-resolution cameras, as well as point and shoot cameras and digital SLRs with increasing resolution and lower costs.

A couple of the brands offering these are Bushnell and Zeiss and these are quite good.

Courtesy of Zeiss

Specialized Riflescopes

Red Dot (Reflex) Sights

These electronic sights were designed and offered in the mid-1970s by Aimpoint as a product for close range use with zero magnification (called 1x). They are quick to aim and get off a shot fast. Since the initial models appeared, there have been improvements and new features offered by many brands.

© Aimpoint

The red dot is projected onto a screen in the finder and if you see the target, you should be able to hit it.

Red dot sights are useful when mounted to rifles, shotguns and handguns. Users are hunters, target shooters, military and law enforcement.

Courtesy of Truglo

Most of these sights are with a bright illuminated "red dot" which replaces the crosshairs. With some more recent models, additional colors are available. The "dots" are illuminated LEDs which are powered with inexpensive batteries. The dots normally have varying types of adjustable brightness. The size of the dots can range from 2 MOA to 6 MOA.

Some of the main features are – unlimited field of view allowing use of both eyes, unlimited eye relief, no or minimal parallax, windage and elevation adjustments, compact size and light in weight.

There are dozens of brands with hundreds of models available in the market.

In recent years, several manufacturers have been offering 2x to 4x magnifiers to use with the red dots to increase the usable range.

Holographic Sights

Holographic sights came on the market in late 1990 and developed by EO Tech. They are similar to and used for the same applications as the red dot sights with the major difference being the red dot replaced by a holographic reticle.

The user is looking through an optical (glass) window and sees a reticle image (hologram) which is super-imposed at a distance on the field of view that you are looking at. The hologram as seen on the reticle is built-in to the window and the illumination is by a laser diode.

Courtesy of EO Tech

The reticle allows for much greater use and flexibility as compared to a simple red dot as the reticle on the holographic sights are available in many different forms for particular applications.

Laser Rangefinding Riflescopes

Riflescopes with built-in rangefinders are available from a few companies – namely Burris, Bushnell and Zeiss. The combination riflescope and rangefinder is more accurate than using riflescope reticles and is a good evolution in technology.

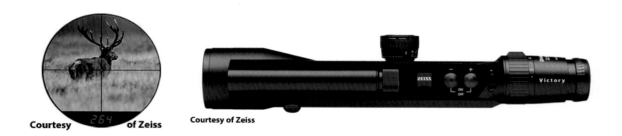

Courtesy of Zeiss   Courtesy of Zeiss

These riflescopes are expensive but for those that can afford them they are a great product and make hunting a little easier when you have the accuracy of the laser rangefinder.

Night Vision Riflescopes

Night vision riflescopes have the ability to see in low light conditions and in total darkness.

The technology is the same as with night vision binoculars discussed earlier.

Courtesy of Pulsar

Night vision riflescopes are useful to hunters in many parts of Europe where hunting is legal at night. They are useful for the military and law enforcement agencies for various applications.

A few of the more popular brands are ATN, Pulsar and Sightmark.

Chapter 7 How to Expand Your Usage of Sport Optics

You may purchase your binocular or spotting scope initially for a particular usage whether it is bird watching or hunting or other activities. However, once you have the basic tool, you may want to expand your horizons at some point in time. The brief list of applications at the beginning of the book can give you some ideas but here are a few of the more popular activities.

Our world is a fantastic place to continually enjoy and as an old saying goes "stop and smell the roses (or flowers)" and optics allow us to expand upon this. With increased concern for our environment, take a closer look with binoculars or spotting scopes at what you have been missing and see why we should preserve as much of it as possible.

Courtesy of Zeiss

Birding – If you are not a birder, consider becoming one at whatever level. Bird watching runs the spectrum of simply enjoying birds in your own backyard or nearest park, to long and difficult high mountain hikes, to the very serious birders who receive an email, text message, or phone call of a rare bird sighting half way around the world and they are on the next airplane regardless of the cost.

Casual birding can be fun and it does not have to be expensive! Most of us have had an interest in birds since we were children as they are wonderful to observe and give us a sense of tranquility. We all look at birds but so much more detail is available to us when looking at them with binoculars or spotting scopes. I was really surprised about 20 years ago on a trip to the U.K. and seeing how the country as a whole is really into bird watching – everywhere!

All you need to get started are your binoculars or spotting scope and a field guide (special book that helps you identify birds and detailed information about them). A wealth of information is available about birding on the internet, in bookstores, nature preserve offices, and specialty retailers. A list of some of the more popular beginning bird

Courtesy of Michael Freiberg

books and field guides is in an Appendix of this book. Bird watching can be for one or two people or in groups as some of the images on these pages show.

Courtesy of Eagle Optics

For bird watching, I would suggest a small full size binocular (7x30, 7x35, 8x40 or 8x42) to get started. Specific size is a personal choice and a lot depends on where and how you will be bird watching. If you will mainly observe birds in your backyard in bright day light a small 25mm compact may be all you need but if you will observe distant predators or shorebirds you may need a 10x42 or so.

If you need to purchase a new binocular, I would recommend that you spend as much as you can comfortably afford, as it will enhance your initial birding experience. I would recommend a waterproof binocular since many times conditions are damp and wet.

If you want to buy a child a binocular for bird watching, I suggest a six or seven power with an objective lens of 30 to 35mm with a wide field of view as it will be easier for the child to begin observing and finding birds.

Courtesy of Bill Thompson III

Courtesy of Bushnell

Courtesy of Swarovski

Courtesy of Bushnell

Courtesy of Michael Freiberg

Courtesy of Tasco

Kletr/Shutterstock

Courtesy of Bushnell

Courtesy of Michael Freiberg

Courtesy of Michael Freiberg

Astronomy – Another interesting and rewarding hobby is astronomy. I believe that all humans have a latent interest in astronomy. It is a great feeling to be in a dark sky area on a moonless night away from city lights, look up, and see the wonders we have to enjoy – fantastic! Unfortunately, there are masses of people who have never seen a star filled sky.

Courtesy of Astro Works

In a dark sky area, you will see a few thousand stars with your naked eyes. With a binocular, you increase the number of stars seen to over 100,000. Using both of your eyes with a binocular allows more comfortable viewing and is more relaxing than using a telescope.

Adding our second eye allows for up to 40% more contrast and resolution, due to the averaging factor that comes from physiology. Image brightness is slightly brighter, when using both eyes. Binocular Summation is the process by which vision with two eyes is enhanced over that which would be expected with just one eye.

No, you do not need a telescope (but many people will progress to owning one) to enjoy the heavens as even serious amateur astronomers use binoculars quite often. With binoculars and spotting scopes you can enjoy the planets and see Jupiter and some of its moons and Saturn and its rings (with much higher power), study our Moon – your first look at the craters with a low power and small aperture binocular should be quite rewarding, observe star clusters, bright comets, nebulae and galaxies. You can see quite a bit with 7x35, 8x40, 8x42, 7x50, or 10x50 binoculars but of course, with larger apertures much more detail is available.

Higher magnification and larger objective lenses will show you more detail but they come with heavier weight and for most, you need a solid tripod platform unless you are using image-stabilized binoculars. You can go up to 8x56 and 9x63 sizes or so and some people can hand hold these just fine but once you get up to 15x70, 20x80 or larger you really need a tripod. On the positive side, you get much more detail and fantastic views unavailable with smaller aperture and lower magnifications. The apertures go up to 100mm to 150mm but the prices go up quickly for these large apertures. A good all-around 20x80 size is very useful for astronomy and for long distance terrestrial viewing as well.

Courtesy of Tele Vue

Spotting scopes are small, compact telescopes. With a spotting scope of 20-60x80, at 20x the Moon is exciting to look at and boost the power to 60x and see even more detailed views and then see what Saturn looks like – quite spectacular, and you can observe star clusters, bright double stars, comets, nebulae and galaxies as well when you know where to look.

Simple star charts and planispheres will show you where to look and you will find it is easy and fun. You should obtain a small red (LED) flashlight to protect your night vision and make it easier on your eyes when looking at the sky and reading star charts. There are many books on astronomy with binoculars and some of the more popular ones are in the Appendix of this book.

Beginning books on astronomical observing are prevalent in the market and will help you get started enjoying the night sky.

Simple star maps by Celestron

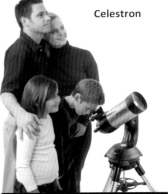

Celestron

You may ask why an amateur astronomer with one or more telescopes would need binoculars. There are several reasons – they are portable and lightweight, they are quick and easy (grab and go) as compared to setting up a telescope, they have a wider field of view and many large astronomical objects look better with binoculars.

Once people get started with beginning astronomy, many get more serious about it and the natural progression is to begin

Courtesy of Astro Works

with a small telescope and then move up to a larger aperture telescope the more serious they become. You can spend a small amount to begin with telescopes but once you get serious you can spend up to $1000.00 or more for a decent size telescope that will allow you to do some very serious astronomical observing and imaging. It is a great hobby!

Courtesy of Warren A. Keller

Courtesy of Tony Hallas/astrophoto.com

Courtesy of Tony Hallas/astrophoto.com

Target Shooting

You may purchase a riflescope for sport hunting. However, if you have never tried target shooting, you should, as it can be exciting.

Courtesy of Bushnell

There are all types of target shooting – normal "target" shooting, trap shooting, clay shooting, skeet shooting, etc.

There are about 7,000 shooting ranges in the U.S.A. alone and the majority of them are outdoor ranges but most are away from large cities and are in rural areas. I am sure there are thousands of shooting ranges spread throughout the rest of the world also. However, as the number of target shooters is large it indicates that people will travel to take advantage of this exciting activity.

There are over 30 million people who target shoot each year. It is a growing activity. This activity can be for individuals or a family activity. The percentage of women target shooters has been increasing rapidly.

© Aimpoint

Many young people get involved with target shooting at an early age and above all else learn how to safely use firearms.

Besides recreational target shooting, competitive shooting of all types encompasses many shooters. It starts in high schools and colleges around the country but mainly in rural areas.

Competitive shooting takes place year round all over the world. Many countries have national competitions as well as worldwide competitions.

Spotting scopes are useful for target shooting in scoring accuracy in competitions as well as just knowing how well you are doing in recreational use.

©AIMPOINT

Some **very general criteria** for choosing spotting scopes for target shooting at various distances are below. Power is a very important factor at the range and high powers must be sharp to be effective. Note there are so many different apertures and powers available:

- 100 yards (meters) – a 50mm aperture (with 15-45x or 18-36x, etc.) is good enough at this distance although a 60mm aperture (15-45x or 20-60x) would provide more details
- 200 yards (meters) – a 50mm may begin to struggle at this distance where a 60mm may be better
- 300 yards (meters) – a 50 or 60mm may struggle at this distance where a 65 to 70mm may be better. A normal quality 80mm (20-60x) will provide better details.
- 400 yards (meters) – I'd suggest a higher end 80mm model with better optics once you get to this distance as a 60mm and normal 80mm models may struggle
- 500 yards + (meters) – this distance is best observed with higher end 80 to 85mm spotting scopes or even 100mm or larger sizes

Courtesy of Shooting Sports USA

Courtesy of Nikon

Chapter 8   Criteria in Choosing Sport Optics

In deciding on a product, there are many factors to consider, including the items below:

• Optical System	• Resolution
• Power	• Prisms (binoculars)
• Objective Lens size and type of Glass	• Optical Coatings
• Field of View	• Near/Close Focus
• Exit Pupil	• Waterproof
• Eye Relief	• Cosmetic appearance
• Reticle (riflescopes)	• Parallax (riflescopes)
• Size & Weight	• Depth of Field
• Brightness	• Contrast
• Light Transmission	• Warranty

Other factors – eyepieces, field lenses, construction, and additional items

Many of the factors listed above (in no particular order) relate in some ways directly to others, and can affect others to some degree. For example, if you increase power (magnification), then the field of view and the eye relief decreases. If you increase eye relief and field of view, then the power decreases. These relationships are general optical rules for the majority of products but if you use very high cost optical components and complex designs you can reduce somewhat the effect of the general relationships.

Metric Conversion

Binoculars, spotting scopes, and riflescopes are mainly from manufacturers in Asia with a minority manufactured in Europe and the U.S.A. and most specifications are in metric form. The following table may be helpful as you read this book if you are not familiar with the metric system and a more detailed table is in the Appendix:

Metric	*U.S. Equivalent*
Millimeter (mm)	0.04 inches
Centimeter (cm)	0.39 inches or 0.03 feet
Meter (m)	39.37 inches or 3.28 feet
Kilometer (km)	0.62 miles or 1093.61 yards
91.44 Meters	100 yards or 300 feet
100 Meters	109.36 yards or 328.08 feet
914.40 Meters	1000 yards or 3000 feet
1000 Meters	1093.61 yards or 3280.84 feet
Gram (g)	0.04 ounces
Kilogram (kg)	2.20 pounds or 35.27 ounces
0.45 Kilograms	1 pound or 16 ounces

Chapter 9   Optics Details

Optical Systems

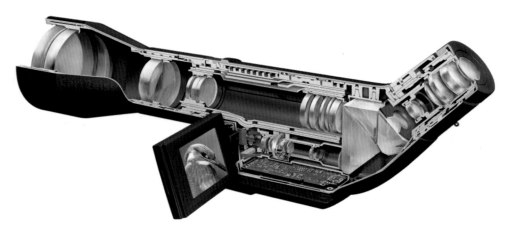

Courtesy of Zeiss

The optical systems of binoculars, spotting scopes and riflescopes are similar. Binoculars use objective lenses, erecting prisms, and eyepieces. Spotting scopes use objective lenses, erecting prisms or erecting lenses and eyepieces. Riflescopes use an objective lens, erecting lenses, and an eyepiece although some high-end units use prisms in lieu of erecting lenses.

20-60x80

Courtesy of Swarovski

The complete optical system is important and not only parts of it. If you have the very best type and grade of optical glass along with a great optical design, it is meaningless if you have a subpar eyepiece or poorly designed erector lenses or prisms. Therefore, all the components of the optics must be designed and built with good materials, precise and accurate manufacturing of the materials, the best technology for fully multi-coated optics and applying them properly, very careful assembly and the detailed and exhaustive end product quality control to ensure performance of the optical system is as advertised and expected.

Courtesy of Zeiss

The optical systems rely on well-made mechanical parts that house the optics and ensure that alignment is good and all parts function smoothly and repeatedly without problems. On very high-end products (Leica, Swarovski, and Zeiss – which I call the Big 3), you should see an image that "pops" out and is super bright with brilliant color fidelity from edge-to-edge. I have experienced this with all three brands many times and it is incredible.

Recently a disturbing thing is that one of these brands is offering much lower cost products with lower quality and I am not sure this is good for their brand image.

About 15 to 20 years ago, there was quite an optical performance gap between the Big 3 and the next level of competitors but that gap has been closing rapidly the last few years from several brands. I will mention several brands (the higher end models of each brand) that to me are surprisingly very good optically on a consistent basis for the cost they sell at – a great value! In no particular order they are – Meopta, Vortex Optics, Nikon, Minox, Celestron, Bushnell, Kowa, and Steiner. There are many more brands just a tad under the quality brands mentioned.

Courtesy of Leica

I have looked through some brands costing about 50% to 70% or so as much as the Big 3, and the views have been very good with only subtle difference in optics but they were very disappointing and I won't mention them here to avoid any potential legal issues.

For the very best optical systems, manufacturers are using a fluorite element or ED (or similar low dispersion) glass in the objective lens. Both are of very low dispersion (the variation of the index of refraction of a transparent substance with the wavelength of light) and both benefit from reductions to chromatic aberration.

Some writers and reviewers note no difference between ED glass optical systems and non-ED glass optical systems as far as chromatic aberration is concerned. However, something is wrong in what they are seeing, as there will be considerable chromatic aberration with any standard achromatic objective lenses versus one with ED glass objective lenses. ED objective lenses should virtually eliminate chromatic aberration unless there is something wrong with the optical design, the glass itself, assembly, or something else.

Fluorite (fluorspar) is a halide mineral made of calcium fluoride (CaF_2) in the form of crystals. Natural fluorite crystals without flaws are microscopic in size. Thus, artificially grown calcium fluoride crystals were developed. The crystals are useful in place of optical glass in very high-end optical systems. Fluorite eliminates all chromatic (color) aberration. Fluorite is very fragile and difficult to manufacture into optical components and these factors are part of why the material is so expensive. When used as an element of an achromatic objective lens, it is normally the inside element (positive) and the other element is of a high dispersion glass as the outer element (negative) facing the outside environment. However, products using fluorite have excellent color fidelity and razor sharp images free of any color aberration. Only a few brands have or are using fluorite in some of their optical systems.

ED is an optical glass of very low dispersion. Over the last several years there have appeared quite a large number of optical products from various brands using this glass in mid to high end prices where the main benefit is (when designed properly as part of the optical system) to help reduce or virtually eliminate chromatic (color) aberration. ED glass, as well as fluorite, can help extend the usability of optical products in low light conditions when normal glass products cannot.

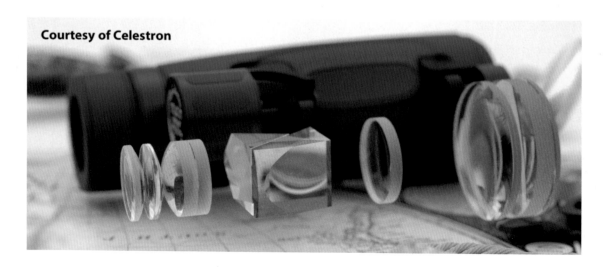

Courtesy of Celestron

Most ED optical glass has traditionally come from Japanese factories such as Ohara and Hoya. In recent years, manufacturing of ED optical glass in China started. A few European countries also manufacture some ED (or equivalent in dispersion) glass.

There are different grades of ED glass that give different levels of optical performance. In general, using better grades of ED glass, in a well-designed optical system, will give you excellent color fidelity and razor sharp images virtually free of color aberration. I say in general because I have seen many binoculars and spotting scopes with ED glass that had quite noticeable color aberration and were not as sharp as they should be due to a lower grade of ED glass or a poorly designed overall optical system.

Courtesy of Leica

In regards to ED, there are some names associated with this – LD, XD, SD, SLD, and UD among others. Fluoride glass is ED glass and not Fluorite (an element) which is generally better for most optical systems but much more expensive than ED glass.

Some companies call their products HD or UHD and other names meaning high definition or ultra-high definition but these, in general, are not ED glass as high definition doesn't really have a meaning and does not compare to fluorite or ED optical glass in low dispersion – don't be fooled!

I might add that you could also use an APO (apochromatic) lens design for the objective lens. An APO optical design traditionally has three elements (triplet) of different types of glass to greatly reduce or eliminate chromatic (color) aberration. However, due to optical design technology advances and lower density glass availability, two element APO designs can be about as good as triplets or fluorite if the very best grades of ED glass are used.

Power (Magnification)

Power (Magnification) is very similar with binoculars and riflescopes. The basic difference is you handhold binoculars while riflescopes are mounted onto rifles or pistols.

Binoculars – the power of a binocular means the degree to which the object or subject you are looking at is enlarged. For example, with an 8x42 binocular, the first number (8) is the binocular power and this type of binocular is a fixed power binocular of which most binoculars are. Virtually all binoculars sold have the power indicated on the binocular. A binocular of 8 power enlarges (or magnifies) the image eight times the size as seen by the normal, unaided human eye. You can also look at it as if the image were only $1/8^{th}$ of the actual distance away. If the object you were looking at were 800 feet (244 meters) away, with an 8x binocular it would appear as though it was only 100 feet (30 meters) away.

8-16x42   Courtesy of Weaver

There are zoom binoculars where you can vary the power. For example, an 8-24x50 binocular means the power is variable between 8 and 24 and anywhere between. In general, low cost zoom binoculars do not perform as well as fixed power binoculars. A few higher end zoom binoculars do perform quite well compared to fixed power binoculars. High zoom magnifications become increasingly more difficult to hold steady and are bigger, heavier, and more costly than conventional binoculars. Zoom models typically have narrow fields of view.

A tip on focusing zoom binoculars – always focus at the higher power first and you will not have to focus as you reduce power. In my opinion, I would not recommend zoom binoculars due to many inherent design problems.

A few higher end binoculars have dual magnification that allows the user to switch between two powers.

More power does not mean better. How much power you need depends on several factors.

Binoculars having powers over 10x usually require mounting to a photographic/video tripod for stability unless they are image-stabilized, as they are too hard to handhold. However, some people have very steady hands and can hold 12x or up to 20x binoculars ok depending on the weight, size, etc.   In general, high powers are limited to specialized areas of interest such as astronomy, long distance observing, or for surveillance work.

Keep in mind that power affects brightness and the lower the power (with a larger exit pupil), the brighter the image and generally the wider the field of view.

Personally, I generally prefer a lower power as I enjoy the brighter images with good detail and a wider field of view. The only exceptions for me are when looking at vast distances or in low light conditions where higher power will pick up details that the lower power will not.

Courtesy of Eagle Optics   **10x42**

In general, increasing power will reduce field of view.

Below is an image of a bird (©mircea bezergheanu/Shutterstock) and how it would look with your naked eye and then how it would look using various powers with binoculars.

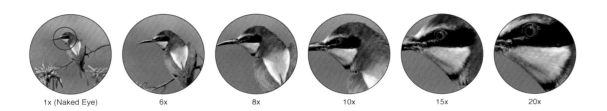

Spotting Scopes – the power of a spotting scope means the degree to which the object or subject you are looking at is enlarged. For example, with a 15-45x60 spotting scope, the first number (15-45) is the spotting scope zoom power range (15x to 45x and any power between). This type of spotting scope is called a zoom (or variable) power spotting scope of which most spotting scopes are.
Virtually all spotting scopes sold have the power indicated on them.

A spotting scope of 15 power enlarges (or magnifies) the image fifteen times the size as seen by the normal, unaided human eye. You

Courtesy of Vanguard

can also look at it as if the image were only 1/15th of the actual distance away. If the object you were looking at were 500 feet (152 meters) away, with a 15x spotting scope, it would appear as though it was only 33 feet (10 meters) away.

There are some fixed power spotting scopes. For example, a 15x50 spotting scope means the power is fixed at 15x. Fixed power models are simple to use, as there is no power changing mechanisms, etc. However, most people prefer to have the ability to change to higher powers to zoom in on certain subject matter. Fixed power scopes have become less common over the last decade or so as the zoom eyepieces used in spotting scopes have become much better in optical quality. Most zoom eyepieces on spotting scopes of the medium to high-end price range are every bit as good as fixed eyepieces at the same power.

A few spotting scopes have interchangeable eyepieces which change magnification that allows the user to choose which ones to use under different circumstances. For example, some of the eyepieces are very low power – 10x or so and have a very wide field of view and long eye relief, then there are mid power eyepieces, there are high power eyepieces for seeking details at long distances and there are special wide angle eyepieces to achieve a wider field of view, etc. The interchangeable eyepieces should be parfocal, which means the image keeps a sharp focus when changing eyepieces without having to refocus.

With the high powers that spotting scopes have, they must be attached to sturdy tripods to achieve good, steady views when observing objects. Flimsy tripods will make for blurry views due to shaking and vibration.

Keep in mind that power affects brightness and the lower the power, the brighter the image (although objective size, exit pupil, and type of coatings also affect brightness).

Personally, I generally prefer a lower power (with similar objective lens diameter) as I enjoy the brighter images with good detail and a wider field of view. The only exception for me is when looking at vast distances where a higher power will pick up details that the lower power will not.

In general, increasing power will reduce field of view and eye relief. Keep in mind magnification also magnifies everything between you and your subject so atmospheric conditions affect the overall image quality.

25-50x82

Courtesy of Leica

18-55x65

Courtesy of Celestron

Below is an image (©tonyV3112/Shutterstock) of a museum and how it would look with your naked eye and then how it would look using various powers with spotting scopes.

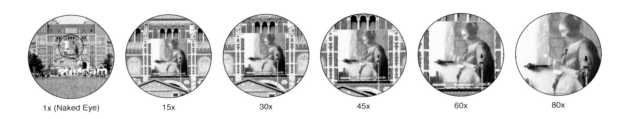

1x (Naked Eye)   15x   30x   45x   60x   80x

Riflescopes – the power of a riflescope means the degree to which the object or subject you are looking at is enlarged. Riflescopes have many different types of powers for different applications in hunting and target shooting and variations within each.

There is an enormous range of riflescope powers available for your decision-making. The power such as a 4x32 (first number defines the power and the second number defines the objective lens diameter in millimeters) is called a fixed power riflescope. Then, a 3-9x40 is called a variable type, which magnifies from 3x to 9x and anywhere in between. The variable power riflescope type is the same as a zoom power binocular – same function but with a different name. There are big riflescopes, compact riflescopes, variable (zoom) riflescopes, fixed power riflescopes, long distance riflescopes, short distance riflescopes, varmint riflescopes, air gun (those with double recoil action requirements) riflescopes, etc.

1. Fixed Power – the 4x32 means the object is magnified 4 times as compared to the naked eye. The higher the number is, the greater the magnification. If the subject you were looking at were 400 yards (365.8

4x32

Courtesy of Konus

meters) away, looking through the 4x riflescope would make the subject appear as though it was only 100 yards (91.4 meters) away. If you were sighting in at a whitetail deer at 100 yards (91.4 meters) away, it would appear to be just 25 yards (22.9 meters) away.

Fixed power riflescopes were the standard for generations. Starting in the 1970s the variable power type became more popular each decade and today greater than 83% of all riflescopes are of the variable type. The fixed power models are heading toward oblivion other than for some specific uses (military sniping, high power target shooting, hunting with .22 caliber rifles, etc.).

Some people prefer the fixed power riflescope for a number of reasons – lighter in weight, no adjustment for power, they are shorter, less complex, more reliable, sturdier, and less expensive and have brighter images (they have fewer lenses). The main negative of fixed types is they have limited versatility. I have used 4x and 6x fixed power riflescopes and like them for the same reasons above.

With a 4x riflescope, you can see clearly enough to shoot deer size game up to 400 yards (366 meters).

A 2x riflescope is common for riflescopes on handguns and on many shotguns for close range deer hunting or for turkey and pheasant shooting.

2. Variable Power – the popularity of variable magnification riflescopes has been mainly due to their versatility. This means you do not have to change riflescopes for different types of hunting and/or in different environments.

In the early years of variables, they were not very durable as compared to fixed riflescopes. However, over the years, technology changes have allowed them to become every bit as good and rugged as fixed riflescopes and the versatility is a great plus.

10-40x50

Courtesy of Barska

For a 3-9x40 riflescope, this means you can vary the magnification from 3x up to 9x and anywhere in between. The power you choose depends on the type of hunting you will be doing. Deer, elk and similar game can be good targets at 400 yards (366 meters). This size riflescope is great for all around hunting.

Sizes of 3-10x, 4-12x, etc. are very useful where the lower power ranges may be good for rabbits or coyotes and the higher powers useful for mule deer and antelope in open country with long distances and dim light.

Below is an image showing a deer (©Gucio_55/Shutterstock) and how it would look with your naked eye and then how it would look using various powers of a riflescope.

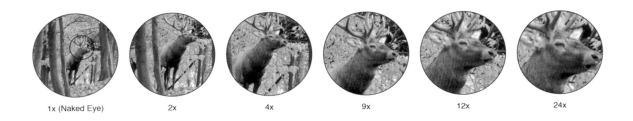

1x (Naked Eye)   2x   4x   9x   12x   24x

Sizes of 4-16x, 6-24x, 8-32x, etc. are useful for small varmints and prairie dogs at long distances where the high magnification is very useful. These are also good for high power target shooting.

Sizes of 1-4x, 2-7x, etc. are useful for bear and other large, dangerous game as well as deer in wooded areas where you need rapid target acquisition and a wide field of view at close range.

1.5-6x42

Courtesy of Explore Scientific LLC

In general, keep your riflescope at low power for encountering game up close or moving while in forests or cover where you need a wide field of view and a bright image. You can always dial up the power for longer distances in clearings or prairies when necessary.

Note that air guns with dual-recoil spring pistons need special riflescopes to handle this tough requirement. However, many standard riflescopes are built today that can handle this.

The normal zoom ratios for years have been 3 times or 4 times (example 3-9x or 4-16x). However, the trend has been to increase zoom ratios of up to 6 times or more but these higher zoom ratios cost more money.

Even though the trend over the last several years has been to go to higher and higher powers, this does not mean it is good. Extremely high power amplifies rifle movement as well as heat shimmers. When at the high powers the images are not as bright, the field of view is narrow, depth of field decreases, target acquisition is more time consuming, eye relief is more critical, etc. If your riflescope is set at the higher powers, you can easily miss a close shot, as you cannot react fast enough.

Objective Lenses

The objective lenses of binoculars, spotting scopes and riflescopes are the front lenses (facing front when looking through the products). Objective lens diameter is normally in millimeters. For example, in a 8x42 binocular, the number "42" is the diameter of the objective lenses. For a riflescope, the 3-9x40 is a variable type where the number "40" is the diameter of the objective lens.

Objective Lens

Virtually all sport optics products have the objective lens size indicated on the products.

Binoculars and spotting scopes have their objective placed in the front body whereas with riflescopes, they are in the objective bell (front cell or housing).

The purpose of the objective lenses is to gather incoming light and form a sharply focused image of distant subject matter.

In general, the larger the objective's diameter, the more light the binocular, spotting scope or riflescope gathers and the brighter the image is with higher resolution and more detail and sharpness. However, more added light is only beneficial to the extent you can use it. These effects are most pronounced under low light conditions (dawn, dusk, overcast day, thick forest), or nighttime use. Keep in mind larger objectives add weight and cost.

Objective Lens

Image Courtesy of Leupold & Stevens, Inc.

The term "light gathering ability" applies to objective lenses (their surface area) especially when comparing different sizes. If you double the size of the objective lens, you quadruple the light gathering ability. For example, a 7x50 binocular has just over twice the light gathering ability of a 7x35 binocular and has about four times the light gathering ability of a 7x25 binocular. Galileo came up with the formula below for refracting telescopes:

$$\pi \times \text{diameter of the objective}^2 \div 4 \quad \text{or for simplicity} \quad \text{objective lens}^2$$

For the example above, $50^2 = 2500$, $35^2 = 1225$ and $25^2 = 625$

For a spotting scope example, let us compare a 15-45x50, 20-60x60, and 20-60x80. If we use 30x to make our comparison, we see that the 60mm has about 44% more light gathering power than the 50mm the 80mm has about 155% more light gathering power than the 50mm and the 80mm has about 78% more light gathering power than the 60mm.

Objective Lens

Courtesy of Tasco

Current trends lean towards larger and larger objectives in riflescopes – 56mm, 60mm, or even 75mm. In most cases, this is not a good choice (in my opinion) due to the large increase in weight. They also require much higher rings and make it extremely difficult to look directly through the center of your riflescope every time and they do not withstand recoil as well – a lot of negatives. For hunting in Europe and Scandinavia, larger objective lenses (normally 56mm) are quite useful for hunting at night, which is legal in many countries.

Most high quality binoculars, spotting scopes, and riflescopes utilize two-element, achromatic objective lenses. The two elements are of different types of glass to help minimize color errors, and do a decent job of this, but a two-element glass combination cannot eliminate the color errors, unless ED glass or a fluorite element is. The color error (chromatic aberration) details are discussed in Chapter 10.

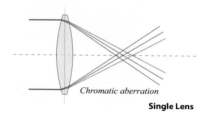

Chromatic aberration

Single Lens

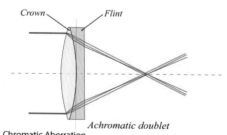

Chromatic Aberration

Low Dispersion Elements – many higher end products use ED (low dispersion) optical glass and a few use Fluorite (crystal) as one of the elements in the objective lens. Dispersion is a measure of the spreading out of the three basic colors from incoming light through the objective lens, which attempts to focus them to one single point. Standard two-element glass cannot do this but with low dispersion elements (ED glass or Fluorite), you can.

You can eliminate chromatic aberration with well-designed apochromatic lenses. The three colors will coincide at a single focus point.

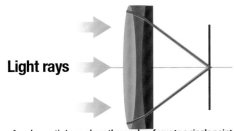

Light rays

Apochromatic Lens where three colors focus to a single point

If the optical design is good, using ED glass or a Fluorite element will give you excellent color correction and razor sharp images all of which add to better contrast and being able to obtain the highest level of resolution for the particular optic.

While enhancing the optical system, ED glass virtually eliminates chromatic aberration (assuming the optical design is good and the ED glass is of the higher grades) while a Fluorite element completely eliminates chromatic aberration. Some writers say that just using ED glass eliminates chromatic aberration and this is not true. The same applies not only to binoculars and spotting scopes but to riflescopes as well.

Many people believe that only the center of the field of view needs to be sharp but it is far more enjoyable to see the complete field of view as one sharp image with reduced chromatic aberration.

The ED glass or fluorite element design advantages really show up under low light conditions whether you are birding or hunting as you can see more detail than you can with standard glass which extends your birding and hunting time. However, beware, not all ED optical products perform as well as advertised due to design flaws, poor manufacturing, or the use of inferior grades of the ED glass itself.

Be aware of what many companies call "HD" for high definition. At times, you are led to believe you are getting low dispersion glass (like ED) but that is not what you are getting.

On mid and high-end optical products, it is helpful to have the rims of the objective lenses blackened to prevent internal glare, which should be a standard manufacturing process.

Eyepieces

The eyepieces (oculars) for binoculars and spotting scopes are the lenses closest to your eyes. They enlarge (or magnify) the image formed from the objectives after it has passed through the prisms of the binoculars or spotting scope. They generally consist of three to six optical elements or more.

Eyepiece

In riflescopes, the eyepiece is similar and enclosed in the eyepiece housing. The eyepiece focuses (see adjustment controls) on the reticle for your particular eye to obtain a clear and sharp image.

Eyepiece

There are many types of eyepieces with many glass types used. **The optical design of the eyepiece is the most important factor about them!** The eyepiece design not only helps determine the quality level but also affects field of view and eye relief. The Kellner (or modified versions) eyepiece is the one most often used. To obtain a wider field of view, the Plossl, Koenig, or Erfle eyepiece is usually used. An Erfle or Koenig has a more complex design and results in a higher cost. There are some complex, multi-element optical designs that are used but with a much higher cost.

On mid and high-end optical products, it is helpful to have the rims of the lenses blackened to prevent internal glare, which should be a standard manufacturing process.

The choice of eyepiece type has a **major** effect on field of view and image quality over that field. In general, the more complex the eyepiece optical design, the wider the field of view with higher image quality. Manufacturers, in general, do not divulge the optical design of eyepieces for sport optics products.

For all optical instruments, the eyepiece should have a rubber eyecup for more comfortable use (rather than hard plastic) and to protect eyeglasses.

Eyepiece

Courtesy of Swarovski

Prisms

Erecting prisms are used in binoculars and spotting scopes as part of the optical design to correct an inverted (upside down and reversed) image. A few specialized riflescopes use erecting prisms but most riflescopes and some spotting scopes use lenses to correct the image. In binoculars, prisms allow compact sizes since they follow a short optical path.

There are two main types of prism systems:

(1) The Porro prism
(2) The roof (Dach) prism

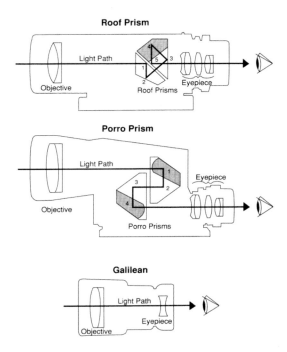

Drawing showing prism designs (Porro and Roof) as well as non-prism type (Galilean)

Which is best is a matter of disagreement. In general, Porro prisms are thought to yield superior optical performance but many roof prisms provide excellent performance if they have phase shift coatings.

Roof Prism   Courtesy of Celestron

Porro Prism

Courtesy of Celestron

Binoculars can give you a 3-D (stereo) type image. The 3-D effect depends on the separation of the lines of sight entering the objectives in Porro and roof prism designs and the distance to the object. Thus, our eyes transmit the images to our brain, which interprets the light coming to it differently when spacing is ideal to give the perceived three-dimensional affect.

Both types can perform well. However, the manufacturing processes (grinding and polishing) and testing are relied on for the prisms to perform up to their potential.

Binocular and spotting scope prisms mainly come in two common styles:

(1) BK-7 and (2) BaK-4

Both types of prisms (BK-7 and BaK-4) utilize high quality borosilicate glass with the BaK-4 using barium oxide as an additive. The only significant difference between the two is the refractive index, n. The BaK-4 has a higher density n = 1.569 and eliminates internal light scattering more than the BK-7 glass (some say this lowers the brightness slightly at the edges) which has a density n = 1.517.

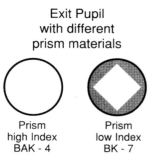

Exit Pupil with different prism materials

Prism high Index BAK - 4

Prism low Index BK - 7

Higher refractive densities are better. BaK-4 prism usage results in higher prices for binoculars than ones using BK-7 prisms. Within these types of prisms are various quality levels and they are not divulged by manufacturers.

BaK4

BK7

Many manufacturers do not tell you the type of prisms used. The use of BK-7 glass prisms can usually be determined by holding the binoculars away from your eyes at a bright light source to see the cone of light coming through. With BK-7s, you will note a diamond shape cutting off a very small part of the light cone (except on very narrow field binoculars) which is shadowed. With the BaK-4 prisms, you generally see the entire cone of light. Thus, the BK-7 has a gray shadow of the light that strikes near the edges of the prisms (mainly in Porro prism binoculars) but that does not translate to a brighter image. One has to also take into consideration the eyes pupil and if it is the same or smaller than the round exit pupil, you have lost nothing.

On some units using BaK-4 prisms, a slight cut-off of the edges (or one edge) is apparent but no noticeable light loss occurs. The prisms being significantly undersized cause this.

Roof (Dach in German) prisms by design are lighter in weight and more compact. They are more complex and difficult to manufacture with more precise tolerances than Porro prisms and thus generally cost more. For example, the angle of the roof apex must be exact at 90° or this can cause severe problems.

The most common types of roof prisms are the Amici and pentaprism. More expensive roof prisms are the Abbe-Konig and the Schmidt-Pechan. The Schmidt-Pechan is more compact and saves some weight, whereas the Abbe-Konig is larger, heavier, and costs more.

In summary of roof prisms, if they are phase coated **and** have dielectric coatings, they are very similar to the efficient performance of Porro prisms.

Prisms (roof and Porro), that are undersize, do not produce complete circular exit pupils and some light may be lost. This effect can also be caused by mechanical obstructions in the light path.

Standard Coatings of Prisms

Many low cost binoculars and spotting scopes have no coatings applied to the rear side of prisms (non-reflective surfaces) and the performance can be ok. Most prisms have coatings, usually an anti-reflection coating such as $MgF2$ (magnesium fluoride).

For reflective surfaces of the prisms, higher end binoculars and spotting scopes have the prisms coated with metallic material such as aluminum (standard or high reflectivity) or silver, which boosts the reflectivity from about 85% for standard aluminum up to 93% to 98% for high reflectivity aluminum and silver respectively. In my opinion, silver is not a good choice since it deteriorates over time. The actual reflectivity results from the coating design and the quality of the application process.

Dielectric Coatings of Prisms

Many roof prisms in the mid to high end price range have dielectric coatings applied. These can boost each surface coating up to 99%+ reflectivity and enhance the overall optical system performance.

Phase Shift Coating of Roof Prisms

         Non-Phase Shift   **Phase Shift Coating**

In roof prisms, due to the nature of light waves, 70% of the light reflected off one roof surface is ½ a wavelength phase shifted from the reflected light off the other roof surface. This causes deterioration both in contrast and sharpness and it affects the resolution as well as color definition. Due to this, Porro prism binoculars have had a slight edge in optical quality. However, many manufacturers offer coatings on the roof with an anti-phase shifting material on binoculars.   Just a few years ago they were available from various brands at a mid to high-end price point but now are available on some brands costing a hundred dollars or more.

The reflected light off the roof prisms is phase corrected (similar) through each barrel of the binocular.

Thus, a phase corrected roof prism binocular with dielectric coatings is equal (not better or worse) to a Porro prism binocular in optical performance assuming all else is equal. By correcting the out of phase shift of light waves, you gain maximum contrast along with higher levels of color fidelity and sharper images.

Field Lenses

A field lens, or group of lenses, in many binocular, spotting scope, and riflescope designs are to help performance. It is important in the optical design as it controls various aberrations by modifying (or

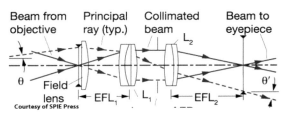

redirecting) the incoming light beams from the objective lens before they are passed on prior to reaching other elements and the eyepiece. The field lens is after the objective lens and prior to the eyepiece. In riflescopes, it allows the erecting lenses to be smaller.

Focus Lenses

In riflescopes, a focus lens is required when the correction for parallax is a side focus type on the left side of the main turret. It works in conjunction with the objective lens to eliminate the parallax at lower powers. When turning the side focus knob it moves the focus lens axially until the reticle is in sharp focus.

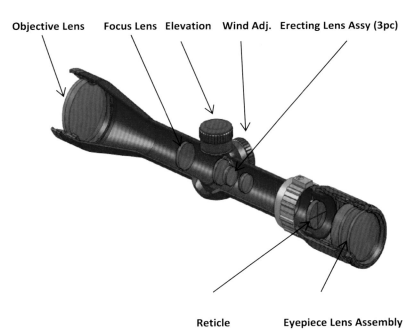

Erecting Lenses

Erecting lenses are required in riflescopes and many spotting scopes. They are the reversal optical system to correct the upside down and reversed image coming from the objective lens. They not only correct the image, they also control the variable magnification, control the positioning of the reticle and provide required eye relief. On mid and high-end products, the rims of the erecting lenses are blackened to prevent any internal glare to ensure throughput transmission efficiency.

Some riflescopes use prisms instead of the erecting lenses. These types are for military and other applications where a more compact size is required but at a much higher cost due to the complexity of the prisms and to properly mounting them securely, etc.

Optical Coatings

Coatings of the optical elements of binoculars, spotting scopes, and riflescopes reduce light loss and glare due to reflection and increase light transmission, sharpness and contrast.

Reflected light is a limitation of sport optics instruments. When light strikes normal glass, 4 to 5% of it is reflected back from the glass surface (glass itself absorbs some light as it passes through). With 10 to 16 or

Optical Coating Machine Chamber with the Computer Control Panels

more glass surfaces in an average binocular, spotting scope, or riflescope, it is possible to lose 50% or more of the light originally striking the objective lens. Worse yet, there is all that reflected and scattered light bouncing around inside your instruments which causes glare and ghost images.

When the surfaces of glass receive a very thin vacuum film of certain metals (usually magnesium fluoride - $MgF2$), then reflected light is reduced to about 1½ to 2% per glass surface. This coating process is an antireflection coating.

Multi-coatings (thin films of metals or other materials) can reduce the amount of reflected light to 0.2 to 0.5% per glass surface and result in a higher light transmission, sharper image and better contrast than standard coatings. Nevertheless, be careful of the

marketing hype from some manufacturers, as they will say they have 99.8% light transmission but they do not tell you that this is per lens surface and not the complete optical system throughput transmission. Please see the section on Light Transmission for more on this.

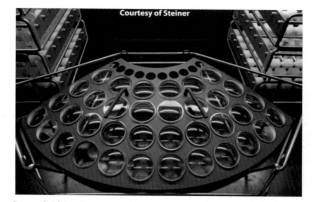

Coated Objective Lenses being removed from the Chamber

Coatings must be uniform in thickness and density or unpredictable reflections and other problems occur. The actual number of layers (from a few to almost one hundred) are somewhat meaningless as the most important factor is the actual chemicals used and the coating design which in most cases is kept secret and proprietary by the manufacturers. Poorly designed and/or applied multi-coatings can be no better than "coated" optics and sometimes worse from what I have observed over the years. In addition, two similar products can have the same fully multi-coated formula but due to glass quality differences there is a difference in the performance.

Many people think they can tell how good coatings are by their color. This is not possible and the color of the coatings can vary enormously by the chemicals and procedures used. Magnesium fluoride color itself ranges from a very pale blue to a deep purple (violet). Multi-coatings can exhibit various colors or multi-colors depending on the angle you are looking at but most have shades of purple, violet, green, or blue but I have even seen them red or even yellow but rarely.

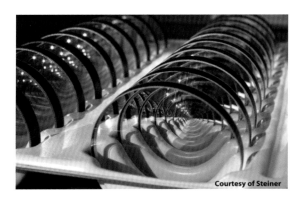
Courtesy of Steiner

Occasionally you will see binoculars or riflescopes designated as having UV coatings. These reduce glare and internal light reflections. They do reject harmful UV light and perform well at high altitudes but do not transmit as much light as multi-coatings.

You may see lower end binoculars with "ruby" coatings where the objective lenses have a bright orange to deep red color on them. Stay away from these! They sell more for the way they look than what you see through them. They give off a bluish tint across the field of view with decreased brightness and thus the image is not very good. About the only thing they are good for is to cut down on bright glare when the sun is reflecting off of snow or water and increase contrast between brown and green objects (deer or other animals against green foliage) but with decreased brightness.

Roof prism binoculars usually have one surface of each prism aluminized (or silvered) which theoretically means that they have more light loss than Porro prism type binoculars but it is insignificant. In more recent years, in some mid and many high-end binoculars, dielectric high reflectivity coatings are applied to give 99%+ reflectivity.

Coatings are one of the most hyped, and in many cases, most misleading specification of sport optics instruments. The various terms are general descriptions for comparison sake:

>*"Coated Optics" (C)* — means that only one or more surfaces of one or more lenses have received an anti-reflective coating

>*"Fully Coated" (FC)* — means that all air-to-glass surfaces have been coated (but in many cases, it means something less). If plastic lenses are used, they are normally not coated

>*"Multi-Coated" (MC)* — means that one or more surfaces of one or more lenses have had coatings applied with multiple films. Some surfaces could be single coated or some not coated at all.

>*"Fully Multi-Coated" (FMC)* — means all air-to-glass surfaces should have received multiple layers of film

I suggest you purchase binoculars, spotting scopes, and riflescopes that are fully multi-coated if you can afford to do it. Light transmission will be higher and the image brighter with more contrast. Most reputable companies offer high quality multi-coatings with various fancy marketing names but the results will be worth it. It does not matter if one  company offers a couple of percentage points of higher transmission than another because you will not be able to detect any difference in usage.

Some brands offer hydrophobic (water repellent) coatings on the outer lenses which prevent fogging by causing condensation from rain, sleet, snow, or even your own breath to bead up into smaller droplets than on normal (or standard) coatings. Smaller droplets scatter less light and result in increased light transmission in these wet situations.

Other brands offer an outer coating that is scratch resistant or protects against oil, dust, smudges, grime, stains, salts, etc.

An Example of Light Loss

A typical binocular, spotting scope, or riflescope with 14 glass surfaces has the following total light loss on average. This is just a very rough average and real light loss can vary considerably depending on many factors.

No Coatings	FC	MC	FMC
47%	25%	20%	5%

From the above, if this binocular were FMC, the throughput light transmission would be about 95%. This is excellent and about the best that is possible. I would be skeptical of firms who advertise much higher rates. Any optical instrument with 90% or higher in throughput transmission is excellent – and any instrument with 85% is very good.

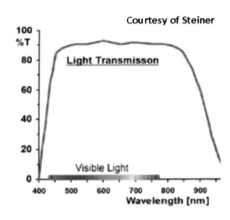

It is unfortunate that many brands advertise very high levels of transmission but they really do not deliver the same thing – I have seen this over the years and proved it with spectrophotometer testing.

Visible Spectrum of the Eye

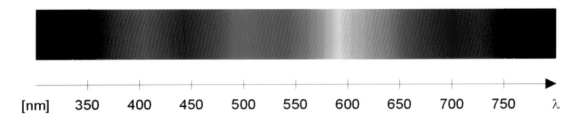

The spectral range shown in graphs is in nanometers (as the above showing 350nm to 750nm) but using Angstroms (Å) is perfectly acceptable and that is what I use most of the time. One Angstrom (Å) = 0.1 nanometer.

The human eye is sensitive to light in the spectral range of 4000Å to 7000Å. Wavelengths below 4000Å and over 7000Å are not visible to the human eye.

Some companies peak their transmission wavelengths closer to the blue range with riflescopes as they say this is best for low light conditions. I am skeptical about this as our eyes (as noted below) are mainly sensitive in the green bands of the visual spectrum and peaking transmission closer to the blue range will render lower contrast levels during daylight hours when most hunting is done. There have been studies made by the U.S. military about small color shifts into the blue range and it is unlikely that object detection or resolution is affected.

Your eye has its peak sensitivity in the green band at 5550Å in daylight and 5100Å in total darkness. Thus for binoculars, spotting scopes, and riflescopes, which are used mainly in daylight, the optical coatings on your instruments should have its peak transmission at the 5550Å point for optimal performance. For astronomical telescopes, used in total darkness, your instrument should have its peak transmission at the 5100Å point for optimal performance.

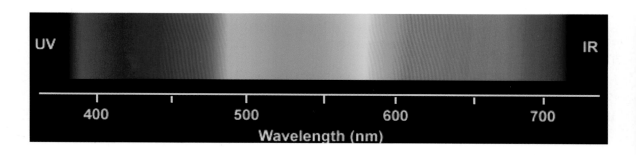

Most optical coatings are broadband type, which covers a wide area of high transmission within a certain wide range. For most optical instruments, the high points should fall within 5100 to 5550Å range.

Field of View

The term means the size, in degrees (called the angular field), of the area you see with an optical instrument. The image you see is circular. For terrestrial usage the field of view is expressed as the width, measured in feet (or meters), of the viewing area you would see at 1000 yards (or 1000 meters) which is called the linear field. For riflescopes, the linear field of view is feet at 100 yards or meters at 100 meters.

If you only know the angular field but want to know the linear field in feet, then multiply the angular field by 52.5. For example, if the angular field is 8°, then 8x52.5 = 420 feet (linear field). In reality, 1° = 52.365 ft. @ 1000 yards but in the industry it is rounded up to 52.5 for easy calculation.

Linear Field = Angular Field x 52.5

For meters, you first need to convert feet to meters and 52.365 feet equals 17.455 meters. Thus, for easy calculation use the following formula where we round the meters to 17.5.

Linear Field = Angular Field x 17.5

Using the above example where the field is 8°, we find using the formula above 8x17.5 equals 140 meters@1000 meters.

The greater the field of view, the greater the area you will see in the image. Greater fields of view are not always better but helpful for birding, hunting, spectator sports, nature watching, hiking and astronomy. For hunting, it is easier to spot game and track moving targets. For other uses, it is important when

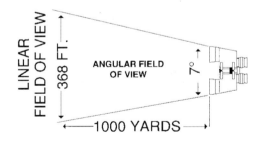

the object observed is likely to move or when you are moving. In general, wider fields usually mean less eye relief and more cost due to the complexity of wide field eyepieces.

Field of view is related to power such that the greater the power (in general), the smaller the field of view.

The diameter alone of the objective has no bearing on the field of view!

Some binoculars are wide-angle models. There are no exact criteria to determine what wide angle is. It is widely accepted that any binocular with eyepieces having an apparent field of view of 65° or more is wide angle according to the Japanese (JS) standard. The Europeans consider 60° as being wide angle according to ISO 14132-1:2002.

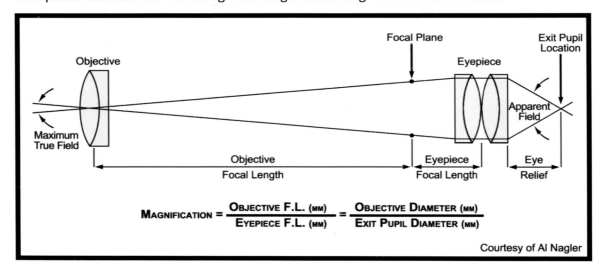

$$\text{MAGNIFICATION} = \frac{\text{OBJECTIVE F.L. (MM)}}{\text{EYEPIECE F.L. (MM)}} = \frac{\text{OBJECTIVE DIAMETER (MM)}}{\text{EXIT PUPIL DIAMETER (MM)}}$$

Courtesy of Al Nagler

The **apparent field of view** is the angle your eye covers from side to side of the subject matter in the eyepiece. The apparent field is:

Approximate Apparent Field = True (Real) Field x Power
Approximate is used since geometric distortion can change the relationship between "apparent" and "true field"

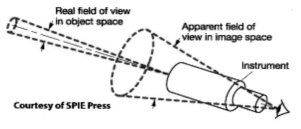

Courtesy of SPIE Press

If we have an 8x42 binocular with an 8° field of view, it has an apparent field of 64° (8 x 8 = 64). There is a newer way of determining the apparent field of view described in ISO 14132-1:2002 but I prefer the traditional method, which is very simple while the ISO method uses a more complex formula, which can be found on line if you desire.

The theoretical field of view of our eyes is 180° (using both eyes). However, in reality we can only see about 140° to 160° as it varies from person to person. As a reference, the full moon is 1/2° across (the same area as a small human finger held at arm's length). When holding your arm straight out and making a fist, this will result in a field of about 9° to 10°.

A 3x-9x variable riflescope might have a field of view at 100 yards (91.4 meters) a bit over 30 feet (9.1 meters) at 3x and around 14 feet (4.3 meters) at 9x.

Eye Relief

Eye relief is the distance a binocular, spotting scope or riflescope is from the eye where you can observe the full field of view comfortably with no dark edges. This optimum position is the eyepoint and the distance from the eyepiece lens (surface facing you) is the eye relief in millimeters.

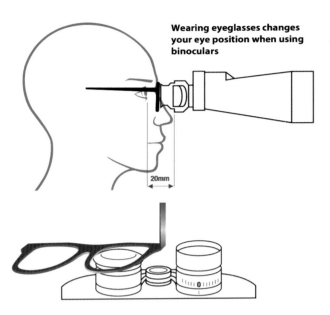

Wearing eyeglasses changes your eye position when using binoculars

For binocular and spotting scope users longer eye relief provides viewing comfort and is especially helpful for eyeglass wearers. The distance from the average human eye to the inside of an eyepiece lens is about 12 to 14mm and this is adequate eye relief for most users who do not wear eyeglasses. It is about another 4 to 6mm to the plane of the binocular eyepiece lens. So for eyeglass wearers (for vision correction or when wearing sunglasses) you need a minimum of 16 to 20mm of eye relief to see the full field of view.

Some manufacturers use the term "high eyepoint" which means long eye relief. Keep in mind that wide angle binoculars usually mean less eye relief.

Eyeglass wearers need longer eye relief but they also suffer from peripheral light loss. It is best (if possible) to remove your eyeglasses when using binoculars or spotting scopes if you do not have astigmatism. If you must wear eyeglasses, then fold down or twist down the eyecups (or other mechanism), if available, to obtain the widest field possible.

If you do not wear eyeglasses, longer eye relief is better since your eye comfort is relaxed, as you do not have to press hard against the eyecups to see the whole field of view. Without eyeglasses, the eyecups should be in the up position. Many binoculars have twist up eyecups that allow you to tweak the position best suited to your eyes.

Riflescopes need much longer eye relief than binoculars and spotting scopes. Heavy recoiling rifles need a minimum of 2 ½" and 3" to 3 ½" or more of eye relief is even better. This is to prevent the recoil action from having the rifle hit your forehead or eye (called shooter's eyebrow or scope eye) and causing injury to you. Remember, increasing eye relief means less field of view.

Courtesy of Meopta

Handgun riflescopes as well as some shotgun riflescopes are designed for very long eye relief (12" to 24" or longer) where the firearm is meant to be held out at arm's length during usage. The down side of the long eye relief is a smaller field of view but they are used for close distances so this is not as critical.

On most zoom-powered binoculars, spotting scopes, and variable power riflescopes, the eye relief will vary with the power – decreasing as power increases. However, more and more variable power riflescopes offer the same eye relief throughout the power range on higher end models.

Be careful if you are near sighted, and wear your glasses when using spotting scopes, as on many models the eye relief may be very short at the high power and cuts off part of the field of view.

You can measure the eye relief with a simple test. Aim the binocular, spotting scope, or riflescope at a brightly lit sky while moving a piece of waxed paper toward and away from the eyepiece. A spot of light will appear on the waxed paper. When this spot's diameter is smallest and the image sharpest and brightest, you have found the eyepoint. Then measure this distance from the wax paper to the eyepiece lens in millimeters.

Near (Close) Focus

Near focus is the closest distance to the observed object that the binocular or spotting scope is useful while retaining a sharp focus.

A binocular or spotting scope specification for near focus is theoretical and based on a young person's eyes. Older people have a more distant near focus. In addition, people in general have a wide variance in their particular eyes and focusing distances can vary from person to person.

Courtesy of Pentax

6.5x21

Eyeglass wearers who remove their glasses when using binoculars and spotting scopes, will generally note a change in near focus. Near sighted people will note a closer near focus and farsighted people will note a further near focus.

Steven Russell Smith Photos/Shutterstock

Many serious birders request a near focus of 6 feet (1.8 meters) or less but for many casual birders (including myself), 15 feet (4.6 meters) is acceptable for most birding applications. For butterfly and insect observers, near focus should be 6 feet (1.8 meters) or closer. The Pentax (shown above) focuses to an incredible 19 inches (49 centimeters).

Some factories use a formula to find the adjustable range of the diopter and divide the square of the power by the positive figure of the measured range. For example, a particular 8x56 binocular has a diopter range of +5.5 to -5.5. Then $8^2 = 64$ which is then divided by 5.5 = about 11 meters or about 36 feet for the near focus. This formula was routinely used many years ago and I believe it was accurate when used for individual focused binoculars and some central focus models but I would not vouch for its accuracy in today's manufacturing.

At low powers with spotting scopes, near focus ranges from 8 feet (2.4 meters) to 40 feet (12.2 meters) or more depending on the optical design. Unless you often look at objects at a close distance, near focus is of no concern.

Palto/Shutterstock

Some binocular repair companies can adjust particular binoculars to have a closer near focus. However, infinity focus can suffer in optical sharpness.

Depth of Field

Depth of field is the distance from the nearest to the furthest objects in the field of view that appear to be sharp. Appearing to be sharp is relative as there can be a wide difference between what different people see and accept. The image of a fawn shows daises and the distances in front and behind where they are in focus is the amount of depth of field.

There are no industry standards and for some people it is irrelevant, as you just refocus at different objects but for others it is important, as they want to use controls less often.

Here are some general observations from my experience looking through hundreds of different optical instruments:

- As magnification increases, depth of field decreases
- As distance increases, depth of field increases
- If you pay more attention to an object, the depth of field decreases
- Eyesight of individuals vary in the amount of depth of field they can detect
- Binoculars with a 6 to 8 feet (1.8 to 2.4 meters) close focus normally have less depth of field at these near distances

How much depth of field is acceptable is a personal decision.

Exit Pupil

Technically, the exit pupil is the image of the objective lens as formed by the eyepiece. Exit pupil is the size (or diameter) of the bright beam of light (in millimeters) that leaves the eyepiece of the binocular, spotting scope, or riflescope.

The diagram below shows incoming light going through the objective and forming an image at the image focal plane. The eyepiece magnifies this image and it is viewed at the exit pupil.

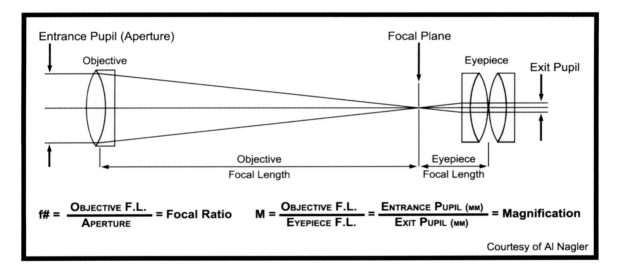

$$f\# = \frac{\text{OBJECTIVE F.L.}}{\text{APERTURE}} = \text{Focal Ratio} \qquad M = \frac{\text{OBJECTIVE F.L.}}{\text{EYEPIECE F.L.}} = \frac{\text{ENTRANCE PUPIL (MM)}}{\text{EXIT PUPIL (MM)}} = \text{Magnification}$$

Courtesy of Al Nagler

The larger the exit pupil is, the brighter the image. However, it is only applicable if the eye pupil is large enough to accommodate it.

Large exit pupils are advantageous when viewing in low light (dawn or dusk, overcast day, thick forest) or at nighttime.

For astronomical applications, the rule has been that the exit pupil should correspond with the dilation of the dark-adapted pupil of your eye, which is between 5 and 9mm (maximum available). This maximum size decreases with age. The eye's pupil size is decreased by smoking, contaminants in the air, poor health, nervous eye movements, dietary habit, and possibly by bright starlight. This same rule applies to binoculars, spotting scopes, and riflescopes in low light.

Different experiments by Lowenfeld and Kornzweig have shown how pupils decrease with age (see the accompanying graph). People of all ages vary tremendously in their pupil size but for most people, the pupil size decreases from the mid-teens on. As we grow older, the dark-adapted pupil grows closer to the same size as it is in bright light. However, there are many exceptions to the experiments.

On a bright day (high noon sun), your pupil shrinks to about 3mm and you would see no difference in brightness between a 3mm and a 9mm exit pupil from your optical product.

Under low light conditions (dusk and dawn or dark cloudy days), your pupil shrinks to about 4 to 6mm.

The Eye's Pupil Size

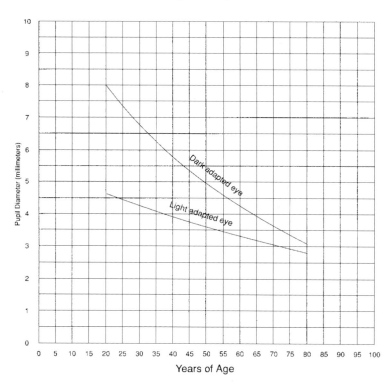

Adapted from Night Vision (National Academy Press, 1987)

If the exit pupil of a binocular, spotting scope or riflescope is larger than the entrance pupil of the eye some light will not enter the eye. The image seen will continue to have the same brightness regardless of how much the size of the exit pupil exceeds the entrance pupil of the eye. The exception is in astronomy when looking at point sources (stars) where the brightness of the star's image is determined by the size of the objective.

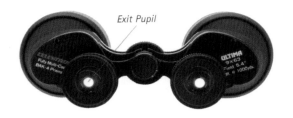
Exit Pupil

When using binoculars in bright light a 7mm or larger exit pupil can be helpful if you are moving or on a boat by making it easier to keep your eyes' daylight-contracted pupil centered in the binocular's larger exit pupil.

With a riflescope, you may notice that you will be able to move and still maintain the image. In other words, the larger exit pupil makes it easier to put your eye where it can receive the light – anywhere in the large exit pupil cone of light and helps avoid vignetting. For hunting, you can quickly find game animals that move rapidly.

You can see the exit pupil (illuminated disc outside the eyepiece) by holding a binocular, a spotting scope, or riflescope out at arm's length and looking toward the eyepieces at a bright light source (bright sky, bright object **but not the Sun**) . You can measure the exit pupil with a metric ruler or scale.

To calculate the exit pupil, divide the objective lens (millimeters) by the power. For example, the exit pupil of 8x42 binoculars is 42 divided by 8 = 5.25mm, with a 20-60x80 spotting scope the exit pupil is 4.0mm at 20x and 1.33 at 60x and with a riflescope of 3-9x40 the exit pupil is 13.33mm at 3x power and 4.44mm at 9x power. An Appendix table shows the exit pupil size of various sport optics instruments.

$$\textbf{Exit Pupil} = \frac{\textbf{Objective Lens Diameter (mm)}}{\textbf{Power}}$$

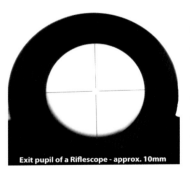
Exit pupil of a Riflescope - approx. 10mm

Generally, exit pupil decreases with greater power (assuming the same size objective lenses). This is the same with zoom binoculars and variable power riflescopes. For example, with a 7-21x35 zoom binocular, the exit pupil at 7 power is 5.0mm and at 21 power it is decreased to 1.7mm and then with a variable power riflescope 2-7x32 the exit pupil at 2 power is 16.0mm and at 7 power it is decreased to 4.4mm.

Brightness

Brightness is the objective lenses (binocular, spotting scope, or riflescope) ability to gather and transmit enough of the available light to the eyepiece to give a sufficiently bright image at the exit pupil for good definition. Brightness also helps in differentiating colors of objects. **The most important item associated with brightness is the size of the exit pupil.**

Brightness is dependent on several factors:

      (a)   Exit pupil diameter
      (b)   Intensity of the light coming from the object you are viewing
      (c)   The type of optical coatings used
      (d)   Transmission and reflection losses of light in passing through the instrument

A few indices are available in an attempt to define brightness. However, all are useless in my opinion, as there are too many limitations, etc.

(1) Relative Brightness Index (R.B.I.)

Several companies use the R.B.I. as a comparison of image brightness but **it does have severe limitations discussed below**. R.B.I. is squaring the exit pupil. In general, larger exit pupils (with all parts of the optical system being equal) can transmit more light.

An R.B.I. of 25 or more is useful in low light conditions. In bright light, an R.B.I. of 51 (7x50 binocular) would have no brightness advantage over one of 10 (8x25 binocular) due to the small exit pupil of the user's eyes.

$$\text{R.B.I.} = \text{Exit Pupil (mm)}^2$$

To calculate the R.B.I. for a 7x42 binocular (or at 7x with a 3-9x42 riflescope), take its exit pupil of 6mm (42 divided by 7). To finish the calculation, $6^2 = 36$ R.B.I.

A limitation of this index is its assumption that all binoculars, spotting scopes, and riflescopes have the same light transmission, which is not true. It also does not consider the quality of the optical system and coatings.

An Appendix lists the R.B.I. for various size binoculars, spotting scopes, and riflescopes.

(2) Twilight Factor Index (TW)

Several companies use the twilight factor as a measurement of viewing efficiency (sharpness) and image detail in twilight (low light) conditions. The larger the twilight factor, the more efficient the low light performance. **This test also has severe limitations.**

To calculate the twilight factor, take the square root of the power times the objective lens diameter (in millimeters). For example, a 7x42 binocular (or at 7x with a 3-9x42 riflescope) has a twilight factor of 17.1. $\sqrt{7x42} = \sqrt{294} = 17.1$

$$\textbf{Twilight Factor} = \sqrt{\textbf{Power x Objective Diameter(mm)}}$$

This formula considers more than the R.B.I. and is a better indicator of brightness. **It has been proven that when observing low contrast subject matter during twilight (not in the dark) higher magnifications will increase contrast and more detail will be seen.**

The problem with the twilight factor is the reverse of the R.B.I. Larger magnifications with larger objective lens diameters will end up with higher values. However, no compensation is considered for light loss with increasing magnifications nor does it take into account that not all binoculars and riflescopes of the same size have equal light transmission. It is useful in comparing different objective lens diameters with the same magnification but is unnecessary since again we know that larger objective lens diameters have brighter images. An Appendix lists the twilight factor for optical products.

(3) Relative Light Efficiency Index (R.L.E.)

Some companies have used this index in the past to take into account the use of new prism materials, new objective lens materials and improvements in coatings, all of which affect the brightness. It is not being used by anyone at this time. Limitations are similar to R.B.I.

$$\textbf{R.L.E. = R.B.I. + 50\% (Compensation for coated optics)}$$

All Indices

All the various indices (R.B.I., Twilight Factor, and R.L.E.) are guidelines used (or were used) by several companies to try to compare the brightness of different sized sport optics products. **Their usefulness is very questionable, unreliable, and misleading.** You want a large enough exit pupil for a bright image with an objective lens that is large enough to provide that exit pupil for the power that you require for seeing details you are seeking. Also to be considered is the type of prisms being used (on binoculars or spotting scopes), the type and quality of glass for objective lenses and eyepieces, as well as the type of optical coatings used.

Light Transmission

Light (throughput) transmission also can mean a percentage of how efficiently light is transmitted through the binocular, spotting scope, or riflescope optical system (from objective lens to your eye). This is very important!

There are many variables that effect light transmission from type of optical design, glass type used, optical coatings design and application, as well as many other items.

Many companies mislead you by publishing a number for the transmission of a single surface and do not tell you the overall transmission through the complete optical system with multiple lens surfaces.

Unfortunately, there are no industry standards for light transmission. The best way of measuring is to use a scientific instrument called a spectrophotometer or with a monochromator.

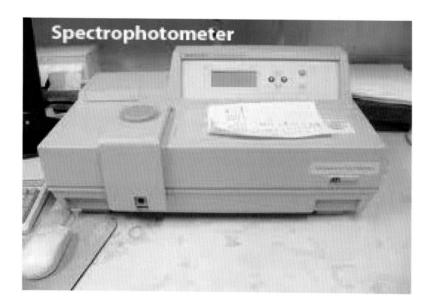

However, for technical types, there is a valid way of estimating throughput transmission. The information is available in *Field Guide to Binoculars and Scopes* by Paul R. Yoder, Jr. and Daniel Vukobratovich. SPIE Press publishes it. This is an excellent book.

Resolution (Resolving Power)

Resolution is the ability of an optical instrument to distinguish fine detail (sharpness). Better resolution also provides more intense color.

The image of owls shows greater resolution in the owl on the left.

Courtesy of Pentax

Resolution varies directly with the size of the objective lens. All else being equal, a larger objective will always deliver more detail to the eye than a smaller objective lens.

Resolution is in seconds of arc. The smaller the number of seconds of arc, the better the resolution will be. The human eye has a resolving power of 1 to 2 arc minutes depending on the study used.

One formula for determining the theoretical resolution of various size binoculars, spotting scopes, and riflescopes is to divide the objective lens diameter (in mm) into 116. For example, the resolution of 50mm diameter objectives is approximately 2.3 seconds of arc (116 divided by 50 equals 2.32).

The accompanying table shows the theoretical resolution of various binoculars, spotting scopes, and riflescopes.

$$\textbf{Resolution} \quad = \quad \frac{\textbf{116}}{\textbf{Objective Diameter (mm)}}$$

Given the resolving power of the eye is about 1 arc minute or so in daylight, the eye can resolve fine details in a chart with black lines and white spaces and subtends to about 2 arc minutes. Thus, using the 1951 USAF resolution chart, 2 arc minutes = 58mm/line part at 100 meter distance or 58x2 = 116 to be used in the formula above.

You can use the USAF resolution chart to test and compare various sport optics instruments. Do the tests at various distances starting at 15 to 25 yards (or meters) and then move further away in increments of 10 yards (or meters) and test again to see how much of the chart can be resolved. For spotting scopes, you may want to start a little further away due to the high powers.

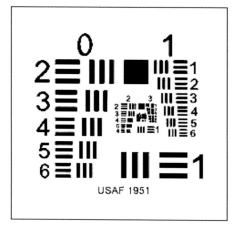

To compare or test for resolution without having the USAF resolution chart, you can use any type of paper monetary currency that is flat without any folds or creases. Attach the currency to a flat wall, fence, tree, or other stable structure. Determine the distance that you can resolve various details on the currency and match these from product to product. You can also do the same tests under various lighting conditions – bright daylight, cloudy day, or low light conditions (dawn or dusk). In low light, the resolving power of the eye decreases to about 4 to 5 arc minutes.

In making comparisons between various products, use the same power.

Keep in mind that these resolution numbers are theoretical. Resolution is the combined quality of the optical components, atmospheric conditions, optical and mechanical alignment, collimation and the visual acuity of the individual.

Theoretical Resolution of Objective Lenses

Objective Diameter- mm	Resolution Arc Seconds		Objective Diameter - mm	Resolution Arc Seconds
14	8.3		45	2.6
15	7.7		48	2.4
16	7.3		50	2.3
18	6.4		51	2.3
20	5.8		52	2.2
21	5.5		56	2.1
22	5.3		58	2.0
23	5.0		60	1.9
24	4.8		62	1.9
25	4.6		63	1.8
26	4.5		65	1.8
27	4.3		66	1.8
28	4.1		67	1.7
30	3.9		70	1.7
32	3.6		72	1.6
33	3.5		75	1.5
34	3.4		80	1.5
35	3.3		82	1.4
36	3.2		85	1.4
37	3.1		90	1.3
38	3.1		100	1.2
40	2.9		120	1.0
42	2.8		125	0.9
43	2.7		127	0.9
44	2.6		150	0.8

Contrast

Cont   objects in the image
"stand out from" or "stand apart from" each other and from the general background.

Higher contrast helps to see fainter objects or subtle detail which is important to serious birders, serious hunters and for amateur astronomers. In the image shown the bird on the left side has a much higher contrast level.

Contrast is dependent on resolution where the finer resolving power, in general, the better the contrast will be. In addition, the better the optical coatings, the better the contrast will be. The suppression of stray light and glare is important to achieve maximum contrast.

Other factors that affect contrast are the quality of the optics (objectives, prisms, field lenses, erecting lenses and eyepieces), quality of manufacturing, collimation, and air turbulence, sharpness of focus and aberrations of your eyes.

Courtesy of Pentax

Chapter 10   Optical Aberrations

In designing optical systems, the optical engineer must make tradeoffs in controlling aberrations to achieve the desired result of the design. Aberrations are any errors that result in the imperfection of an image. Such errors can result from design, fabrication or both. It is impossible to design a perfect optical instrument that is aberration free. Besides any aberrations from the optical design, air turbulence and other environmental factors limit the resolution of optical instruments especially at long distances.

When you buy a binocular, spotting scope, or riflescope, your expectations are that it should be sharp at the center and at the extreme edges. However, in reality this does not happen due to design compromises (except in some high-end products). Some aberrations of a minimal amount are present in all optical instruments and generally are less apparent as the price of the instruments increase. So, do not be too concerned unless the aberrations are severe or bothersome. A few aberrations are briefly discussed below:

Chromatic Aberration – CA (Color Aberration or Color Distortion) — is the failure to bring light of different wavelengths (colors) to a common focus. The result, mainly in a faint colored halo (usually blue or yellow but on rare occasions you can see it in red or green) around bright objects, bright stars, the Moon and planets, or dark objects against a bright sky. Color aberration (CA) is present when looking at telephone wires, poles and straight lines of roofs or buildings especially at the edge of the field but it is actually throughout the field. It reduces contrast, resolution, and color saturation.

Note that purple or blue fringing (seen on the Moon image above) is not CA but color fringing caused by light scatter from a digital camera lens.

In optical products you will see some color aberration when they use achromatic lenses which is inherent in the optical design. Chromatic aberration is reduced in many optical designs using low dispersion objectives (ED glass or fluorite elements).

Carson Optical recently developed a unique CA test.   It uses a chart with blue and red strips that will merge and appear purple when there is Chromatic aberration present.

CARSON OPTICAL'S CHROMATIC ABERRATION TEST

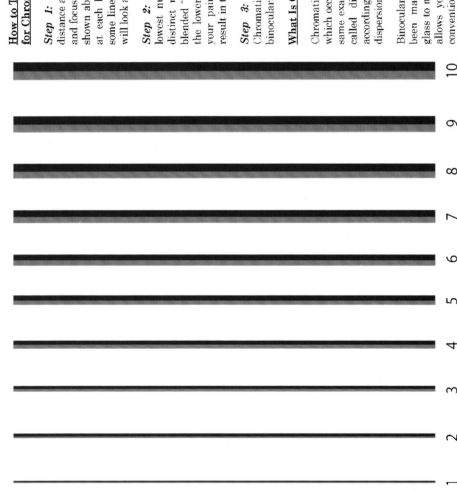

How to Test Your Binoculars for Chromatic Aberration:

Step 1: Place the chart at a distance away, (best results at 50 feet or greater) and focus your binoculars using the black cross shown above. Then use your binoculars to look at each blue/red strips. You will notice that some lines still look blue and red, while others will look as though it is one "purple" colored line.

Step 2: Based upon step 1, determine the lowest numbered line that you can still see distinct red and blue, and not a merged or blended "purple" color. The lower the number, the lower the amount of chromatic aberration your pair of binoculars contains (which will result in the best quality image).

Step 3: Repeat the steps 1-2 to compare Chromatic Aberration between two different binoculars.

What Is Chromatic Aberration?

Chromatic Aberration is a type of distortion which occurs when all colors do not focus to the same exact point, and is due to a phenomenon called dispersion, where light spreads out according to color; some common examples of dispersion are a "prism" or a "rainbow".

Binoculars such as Carson's TD-042ED have been made with ED (Extra-low Dispersion) glass to minimize Chromatic Aberration, which allows you to see more detailed colors then conventional glass.

Innovation In Quality Optics

Distortion — is generally caused when magnification varies from the center of the field to the edges. Looking at an object with straight lines (telephone wires, brick walls, doorframes, etc.) that covers the entire field of view, you will notice a curving of the lines as you look near the edges of the field.

Binoculars, spotting scopes, and riflescopes can have specific distortion called rectilinear distortion and it has two sub types – barrel or pincushion distortion.

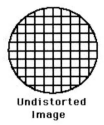

Undistorted Image

Pincushion Distortion

Barrel Distortion

If the lines curve inward, this is barrel distortion, (the most common form of distortion) – where the object magnification decreases with distance from the optical axis and the appearance is of looking at a tradition large wooden barrel.   If the lines curve outward, this is pincushion distortion – where the object magnification increases with distance from the optical axis and the appearance is like a pincushion.

For binoculars and spotting scopes, you want the complete field of view to be free of distortion for higher-end products with the expectation that distribution will be present for lower priced units. For riflescopes, the center of the field is most important but distortion can dampen your overall view and it is annoying to have obvious distortion in your field of view.

Field Curvature/Flatness of Field — caused by the light rays not all coming to a sharp focus in the same plane. The center of the field may be sharp and in focus but the edges are out of focus and vice versa.

All low and mid-priced products have some degree of field curvature. Higher-end products normally have flat edge-to-edge fields due to their having

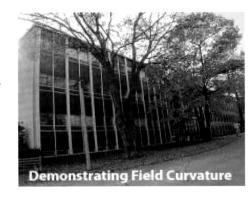

Demonstrating Field Curvature

additional field flattener correcting lenses in the objectives or eyepieces or both.

Again, do not be concerned with these potential problems. Usually, if any of them are severe, you will know it just by using them.

Collimation (Alignment)

The biggest problem with binoculars that consumers have is poor collimation. Collimation is the alignment of the optical elements of the binocular to the mechanical axis. Good collimation prevents eyestrain, headaches, inferior (or double) images and improves resolution.

The manufacturer normally tests binoculars for proper collimation, but some (usually lower priced units) slip by the quality processes. Rough handling or shipping can cause de-collimation. The majority of collimation problems are with Porro prism types but roof prisms can also have this problem.

A high percentage of binoculars sold are out of collimation (mainly the inexpensive units). Most people do not realize this severe problem because their eyes try to compensate for the misalignment.

A couple of quick tests to determine if collimation is okay; First focus on an object in the distance (like a street lamp or sign) about 100 yards or 100 meters or further away. Next, have someone hold a book or other solid object over one objective lens.

Top is good collimation, middle shows vertical collimation errors and bottom shows horizontal errors

Now look through the binoculars (with both eyes open). Have the solid object removed from the one objective very quickly. If two images appear and then blend into one, the binoculars are out of collimation.

Another test is to look at the top of a brick (or similar) wall or roof top at a distance. Looking through the binoculars with both eyes, slowly pull them away from your eyes out to about 12 inches (30cm) in front of you (keep looking through them). At first, you see one view but as the binoculars are pulled away, you will then see two views. These two views should be similar and in line. If one side or the other is higher or lower, you have a vertical collimation problem. If one side or the other is on top of the other, then you have a severe misalignment.

If one side or the other is further apart from each barrel, then you have a horizontal collimation problem, which is rarer than a vertical collimation problem.

If you first look through a binocular and have double images, you need not do any other tests, as obviously something is severely wrong.

There are many articles you can find on the internet about how to collimate your binoculars. I would not encourage you to try them as many do not have the correct information and done improperly can make your binoculars worse. It is true that some people can do a collimation (called conditional alignment) at his or her IPD (interpupillary distance) and the binocular may give acceptable performance but it may not be usable by others, which have different IPDs. The conditional alignment may seem ok for the user but if the optical paths are slightly out of parallelism, your eyes may be accommodating themselves but after observing continually for a long period of time your eyes may become irritated or you get headaches.

If your binoculars are in need of collimation, contact a reputable, independently owned repair facility or factory repair facility. Collimation is very important to how your binoculars perform and they should have the proper collimation machines to do the work.

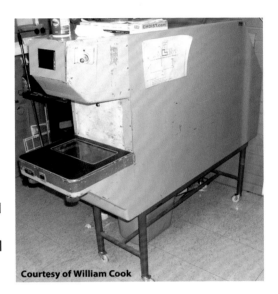

A true collimation is on 3-axes so that the hinge movement (one axis) for different IPDs (extremes of the hinge and mid-point) are all meeting alignment standards for both optical axes. This can only be done with a collimator, regardless of what others may tell you.

Courtesy of William Cook

Further information is available through William J. Cook's SPIE paper (8491-14), *Binocular Collimation vs Conditional Alignment.*

Chapter 11   Controls for Sport Optics Products

Adjustment Controls for Binoculars

Binoculars have a few controls to adjust, set, and use them.

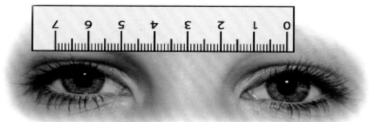

Courtesy of Stingy Specs

Interpupillary (Inter-ocular) Distance – IPD is a term used for adjusting the distance between the eyes (distance between the centers of the pupils) to use binoculars properly. This distance varies among individuals and must be correct to use the binoculars.

A normal range for binoculars is 52mm to 75mm but the range can be somewhat different on certain brands and models or between full size and compacts.

The average pupil distance for adults is about 64.5mm but the distance does vary between men and women and relates to the persons size as smaller IPDs are for diminutive people.

To adjust this distance lift the binoculars up and look through them. Move the two halves of the binocular about the hinge until you see one clear circle of image. Now you are ready to observe.

Some binoculars (mainly Porro prism types) have an interpupillary scale on the hinge, note the setting and it will be faster to set up when using the binoculars again.

Focus Knob Types – there are three basic types of focus systems:

Center Focus

A. *Center Focus* — a central knob (the most common) is used to control the focus mechanism of the binoculars.

Usually the right eyepiece has an individual eyesight adjustment collar (diopter). This permits you to compensate for any vision difference between your eyes.

Some models have the diopter adjustment on the center hinge close to the focus control but unless they have a locking mechanism, they are apt to be moved by accident when focusing. Personally, I prefer the eyepiece type of diopter adjustment as I have used this system for years and like it better.

Several brands have a "click stop" diopter adjustment. You just click to each setting. I do not like these because on many models, the perfect setting for me is between clicks and thus they do not work well for me. Consider also that the setting that works for you may not be at the same click point several years later due to wear of the parts and your best position may be in between clicks.

Some manufacturers offer levers or other devices for obtaining focus faster but these require both hands to focus sharply and they may wear after time. I consider these devices as mainly marketing hype and do not recommend them.

B. *Individual Focus* — allows extra-precise focusing adjustments for image sharpness and clarity since each optical barrel is focused individually.

This type of system is more reliable than center focusing and is used for higher end astronomical binoculars, many marine binoculars and for military use. For subject matter 100 feet (30 meters) or more away with only one person using the binoculars, they are a good choice. For multiple users of the binocular they are not as easy to use due to constant refocusing of both eyes continually.

C. *Permanent Focus* — Jason Empire, in 1988, made a huge commercial success of binoculars that do not need focusing — they are, in essence, "permanently focused". Current units are somewhat better than the early models and a few manufacturers are offering this type of binocular but they are not very popular.

They are extremely easy to use. The negatives to this type of binocular are that there is no way to adjust for vision differences (they have no diopter adjustment) in a user's eyes (near focus eyeglass wearers must wear their glasses) and they do not have a close focusing range for birding and other applications. They can be OK for general viewing and sporting events if you have 20-20 vision or close to it.

Some companies with center and/or individual focusing systems say that once you focus at a certain distance – about 50 to 100 feet (15 to 30 meters) or so away, you now have permanently focused binoculars. They may be pretty close to focus (as any binocular would be) but for critical use in observing objects at various distances, you should refocus for the best sharpness.

Eyepiece and Objective Lens Focusing Methods – you will find advertising of different methods of the eyepiece lenses moving or the objective lenses moving in and out:

> External focus — when turning the focusing wheel, the eyepieces move back and forth.
> Internal focus — when turning the focusing wheel, you cannot see anything move as the lenses inside the binoculars move.
> Objective lens focus – turning the focusing wheel moves the objective lenses in or out.

Many people think the eyepiece internal focus is the best method since the binoculars are exposed less to contaminants. However, the other focus types are very good on most binoculars with the difference being insignificant.

Focusing

Many people think you can just pick up binoculars and look through them and all is OK. Binoculars **must be focused** before using them or you will not get a sharp focus.

Most people have a slight difference between their left and right eyes and the diopter adjustment corrects for this difference. The diopter scale (on some models) indicates the degree of convergence or divergence of the light waves from the binocular.

Center Focus (by far the most popular type) - use the following steps to achieve focus: (1) shut your right eye, look through the left side (eyepiece) of the binoculars with your left eye at an object at least 25 yards (22.9 meters) away. Rotate the center focusing wheel until the image appears in sharp focus; (2) next, close your left eye and look through the right eyepiece at the same object.

Diopter Adjustment

Rotate the diopter control on the eyepiece until the image appears in sharp focus; (3) now look through both eyepieces with both eyes open. Since you have already adjusted the right eyepiece, use only the center focusing wheel to refocus on a new object at a different distance.

Some people advise covering the objective lens of each side with your hand or other object while performing the above focusing adjustment. This way of focusing may be better as your eyes will not have any strain when one eye is closed. However, I prefer the closing of the eye method as I am just used to doing it this way for so long.

Most binoculars have a mark ("0", "Δ", etc.) on the diopter eyepiece and please make note of the setting once you have achieved the best focus, as it will be easier when you have to refocus in the future.

Note: most binoculars have the diopter on the right eyepiece as described above. However, some binoculars have the diopter adjustment close to (or built-into) the center focusing wheel.

Diopter – both eyepieces

Individual Focus - you must close one eye at a time (it does not make any difference, which is first) and rotate the eyepiece until the image is in sharp focus. When changing distances of various objects observed, you must refocus each eyepiece.

Permanent Focus - there is no focus adjustment.

Helpful Hint – if you normally wear eyeglasses for near sightedness and you remove them to use your binoculars, on some models you may not be able to reach a sharp focus at infinity.

Adjustment Controls for Spotting Scopes

Spotting scopes have just a few controls to adjust, set and use them.

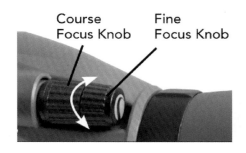

Course Focus Knob Fine Focus Knob

Focus Knob Types – spotting scopes either have a single focus knob or on models that are more expensive there may be a dual focus where one knob is for coarse focus and the other is for fine focus. Some spotting scopes use a "barrel band" focusing system, which is a focus ring that revolves around the body.

In general, dual focusing systems are faster and allow for more precise focusing.

All types of focus systems can work well provided they function smoothly. I prefer the dual focus type as it gives me the comfort that I know when I have "best" focus.

Also, consider how many turns of the focus knob it takes to go from near focus to infinity as the fewer turns the better in most situations.

Helpful Hint – if you normally wear eyeglasses for near sightedness and you remove them to use your spotting scope, on some models you may not be able to reach a sharp focus at infinity.

Zoom Ring

Zoom Magnification (Power) Adjustment Ring – this allows you to change from low to high power and anywhere in between when using the adjustment ring that operates the zoom mechanism. The ring is normally marked showing the magnification at various points.

The ring should take some effort to move it as if it moves too easily it is harder to zero in on the exact magnification you want or it could move easily if you accidently touch the ring and change your magnification.

Courtesy of Vanguard

Interchangeable Eyepieces – this allows for changing eyepieces on spotting scopes that allow this. The eyepieces are held in place by a thumb screw(s), they can be threaded on and off, or they may use proprietary bayonet mechanisms.

Photographic Attachments – there are many ways to take images through your spotting scope, each brand and/or model may do it differently and you will have to see how to do this by looking at your instruction manual. Most of the attachments are optional items but some may be included with certain brands and models.

Taking images through spotting scopes has become quite popular and the common term is "digiscoping" for this activity. There are a couple of ways of doing this:

1. Using a point and shoot digital camera. You can hold your digital camera centered directly behind the eyepiece of the spotting scope and take images. This is not the easiest way to do it, as obtaining focus and holding your camera steady can create problems as you are shooting at high powers. I tried this a few years back a couple of times and did obtain some decent shots but only after a lot of frustration and experimentation.

   The most common way is to use a dedicated or universal digital camera adapter. The adapter will have adjustment controls in both axes, in, and out so that you can center and focus the object quite easily prior to taking images. Make sure you follow the instructions supplied by the manufacturer.

Courtesy of Celestron

2. Using a SLR (Single Lens Reflex) or DSLR (Digital Single Lens Reflex) camera. With this method, you will attach your camera to an adapter. This is accomplished in several different ways depending on the spotting scope you have.

Courtesy of Swarovski

   Some brands use T-Adapters that thread onto the spotting scope (in various ways) and you then need a T-Ring for your particular brand of camera (to install after removing the camera lens) that adapts to your T-Adapter. Some brands have built-in T-Adapter threads and you then adapt a T-Ring for your particular camera.

3. Smart phones can be attached to many spotting scopes and adapters are available from several manufacturers.

Courtesy of Meopta

Courtesy of Meopta

This is quite enjoyable as it expands your hobby. There are numerous articles and information online about digiscoping and I suggest you read as much as possible as there are many techniques to use to maximize the quality of your images taken through your spotting scope.

Sighting Scopes – these allow you to locate objects easier. Some spotting scopes have a low power finder scope or a small "peep" sight to help you. Some spotting scopes have sighting "lines" near the front of the main tube that are helpful in locating your target.

Peep Sight

Tripod – optional tripods have various and controls for tilting, raising or lowering the tripod, moving the tripod horizontally, and various locking features. Various tripods have different types of controls and you will have to refer to the instruction manual for your particular tripod. Make sure you use a stable and high quality tripod that will allow you to take advantage of the spotting scope and provide you with vibration free views or images.

Courtesy of Nikon

Adjustment Controls for Riflescopes

An optical riflescope can have several adjustable controls.

Controls that are near the adjustment turret, close to the center of the main tube body, are for elevation, windage and turret mounted parallax. Controls generally use knobs but some older units can be flat dials with a single slot turned with a coin or a screwdriver and most have caps.

Lockable controls or caps are nice to have so accidental movements are not possible.

Controls are made with a high level of precision in machining and assembly in order that they are smooth functioning with little effort as they can affect accuracy. **They should be repeatable and consistent —after adjusting the dials for different points of impact, when returning to the first setting it should have the same original reading.**

Nightforce

Riflescopes that have hard to turn dials, or have backlash and other issues, can cause the user problems. They should be able to handle operating temperatures from -13° to 155°F (-25° to 68° C).

Most controls have clicks (audible) but some do not. The sound lets you know you have made an adjustment.

Elevation – term used for vertical (up/down) adjustment of your riflescope. You adjust the elevation to zero the crosshairs on the target. This control normally sits on the top of the turret. On a small percentage of riflescopes, the elevation knob becomes a bullet-drop compensator for quick elevation adjustments for long-range shots.

Windage – term used for horizontal (left/right) adjustment of your riflescope. It compensates for the rate and direction of the wind. This control usually sits on the right side of the turret.

Turret Mounted (Side) Parallax Control – term that is used for parallax (described fully in Chapter 12) adjustment and it is mounted on the left side of the turret housing. Turning the control moves a focus lens in front of the reticle. This type of parallax adjustment is technically more complex than the AO (Adjustable Objective) type described on the next page and it is more expensive but also more user-

friendly because the dial can be read with a nominal movement of your head. Personally, I prefer this type of parallax adjustment.

Variable Magnification (Power) Adjustment Ring – allows you to change from low to high power and in between when using the adjustment ring that operates the zoom mechanism. The ring is normally marked showing the magnification at various points.

The ring should take some effort to move it because if it moves too easily it is harder to zero in on the exact magnification you want or it could move easily if you accidently touch the ring and change your magnification.

Focusing – term used for the procedure of focusing the eyepiece (ocular). Some users do not know that a riflescope must be focused to get a very sharp and clear image of the subject on the reticle. Each riflescope needs focusing for your particular eye. Some people write about and believe that eyepiece focusing has something to do with correcting for parallax but this is not true.

Many riflescopes have an eyepiece-locking ring. Unscrew the ring a few turns and then turn the eyepiece itself as you look at a distant object (preferably use a sign or other distinctive subject matter) through the riflescope. Several turns may be needed, but once your object is in sharp focus, screw the locking ring back into its locked position.

Focus Ring

Barska

Most riflescopes today have a fast focus ring (called fast focus) at the very rear of the eyepiece that has gained momentum over the last decade. You normally use less than a full rotation to find the sharp focus position. This is the easier type of focus system.

A hint when focusing – to achieve the sharpest focus, go beyond the point you believe is the best focus and then return slowly back to the best focus position. You do this because sometimes we do not recognize the sharpest focus position until we go just beyond it. To check focus, point your riflescope at the sky or a blank wall (50 to 100 yards or meters away) at its highest power and focus the eyepiece until the reticle is in sharp focus.

Focus may stay very sharp during your usage of the riflescope but you will generally have to refocus when changing to high magnification and changing target distances.

Adjustable Objective Parallax Control – term used for parallax adjustment, which is a rotatable collar near the front (objective end) of the main tube that when rotated moves the objective lens in and out. It is called "AO" or "A/O" which stands for adjustable objective lens and used for adjustment of parallax.

Alpen

Note that both types of parallax controls show distance numbers. However, they are only a guide and not exact settings. Many experienced optics writers note that at low power these controls do not make sense and add weight, bulk, and expense to the riflescope.

When using either type of control, make sure to focus the reticle prior to adjusting the AO or turret to ensure a sharp overall focus.

When first using a riflescope with the above type of controls, turn the dials all the way one way and then the other while counting how many full and partial turns it has. Then cut this number in half, which is the middle, and this is where your adjustments should start and make it easier to use the dials.

Most good quality riflescopes will move the point of impact when you adjust the dials without having to "settle in". Poorer quality riflescopes may need to be shot a few times first to "settle in" the internal adjustments – some old timers tap their riflescopes with a coin or cartridge case that they feel helps this process.

Reading the Dials

For the elevation and windage knobs, the adjustments are put into fractions of "minutes of angle" or "minutes of arc" with both abbreviated as "MOA".

If you do your hunting and rely on click adjustments, their accuracy is vital to your success.

Both terms of MOA refer to a 1/60th division of one degree of arc (1/60°), known as a "minute". As the total piece of a full circle, a minute would amount to roughly .0046 percent of it or 0.0166°.

1 MOA @ 100 yards is 1.0472 inches. MOA changes with distance so it is not a set measurement.

Modifying the standard binocular field of view formula at 1000 yards – a single minute of angle/arc subtends about 1 inch (rounded but 1.0472 is closer to the real number) at 100 yards.

Therefore, the MOA linear relationship for various distances is 1" @ 100 yards or ½" @ 50 yards, 2" @ 200 yards, 3" @ 300 yards, 4" @ 400 yards and 5" @ 500 yards.

The 100-yard distance is the traditional distance on many target ranges.

Note that on some high-end riflescopes, they use SMOA (shooters MOA) where they use 1MOA = 1" and thus be careful of your calculations.

Fractional divisions on the adjustment dials for each click or graduation on the dial can be from 1/8 MOA to 1 MOA but most riflescopes are 1/4 MOA. Some users call this the "click value". This click system makes zeroing and adjustments much easier.

The adjustments must be repeatable. An example with ¼ MOA, one click will get 1/4th movement at 100 yards and four clicks should get you 1" of movement at 100 yards and this should be repeatable at all times at different distances.

Chapter 12   Riflescope Details

Riflescope Tubes

The main body of a riflescope is the "tube".

Riflescope Tube Diameter

There is two main tube diameters in the marketplace plus a few other sizes:

30mm tube on top and 25.4mm (1") tube on bottom

A. The more popular 1" (25.4mm) diameter – called by many the American tube

B. The less popular 30mm (1.18") diameter – called by many the European tube

C. A small quantity of tubes are offered in 34mm, 35mm, or larger diameters for specialized applications

What are the Differences between the 1" (25.4mm) and 30mm (1.18") Tube Diameter?

Overall, there is not much difference:

A. Optically – there is a misconception among many in the hunting industry, including many writers, that all 30mm tubes allow more light through the riflescope, give you a larger field of view, increase light transmission in low light conditions, give you sharper images, etc. However, these comments are somewhat misleading (they do make for good marketing copy!) and in virtually all cases the image you actually see with the 30mm is no different from that with 1" tubes!

   You absolutely have the same field of view, as no larger field of view is possible! The resolution of the image will remain the same in virtually all cases!

   As far as getting any additional light through the system, it depends on the exact optical design of your riflescope. Let us assume for the two tube sizes that the objective size (40mm) and its design as well as the eyepiece design are identical and the variable power is 3x to 9x. The actual exit pupil is 13.33mm at 3x and 4.44mm at 9x and let us also assume the optical coatings are identical.

(1) If the riflescopes both have identical erecting lens systems and do not have a field lens, then the larger 30mm tube will not gather any additional light.

(2) If the 30mm tube has a larger erecting lens system than the 1" tube and neither has a field lens, then the 30mm tube may gather some additional light from the rays passing through the objective lens that were vignetted at the edge of the field of the 1" tube. Note that most 30mm tubes in the marketplace do not have larger erecting lens systems.

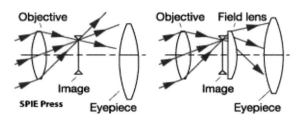

Vignetted rays on the left and captured on the right

(3) If the riflescopes both have identical erecting lens systems and do have a field lens (that refocuses the light rays from vignetting as much), then the larger 30mm tube will not gather any additional light.

For # 2 above, the additional light gain will not be noticeable at all in daylight as the exit pupil at low or high power is larger than the entrance pupil of your eye (depending on the brightness of the day it ranges from 2 to 3mm). The additional light gain in low light conditions (dusk and dawn) could benefit some younger people but I am not sure if they really can see any difference and for older people with smaller entrance pupils there probably is no benefit that can be seen.

Therefore, I am skeptical that spending additional money for a larger 30mm tube mainly for optical improvements makes any sense.

B. Mechanically – the 30mm tube diameter does add rigidity and strength (assuming the same wall thickness as the 1" tube) due to the larger cross-sectional area along with larger rings and mounts.

The 30mm tube does increase the adjustment range for elevation and windage (on most riflescopes) and this is quite useful for long distance hunting.

On the negative side, the 30mm tube is heavier, larger, more prone to dents, and more expensive than 1" tubes.

Most hunters would be hard pressed to detect any performance difference between the two sizes except a little at long distances with added elevation and windage adjustments.

The growth of the 30mm tubes over the last decade has mainly been due to consumer demand associated with marketing hype from the manufacturers.

One Piece versus Two Piece Tubes

One-piece construction is the normal offering in today's market except for some of the lower-end products.   It is stronger, sturdier, and sealed better than two-piece tubes.

Two-piece tubes are generally less expensive to make as assembly time is less and machining is easier.

I would recommend only one-piece tubes due to the higher potential of leaks (gas escaping and water coming in) in two-piece tubes and because they are inferior in strength and structural design.

Tube Materials

Most riflescope tubes are made of aircraft grade aluminum, usually 6061T6. More expensive titanium tubes used mainly in military applications may be slightly lighter in weight than aluminum ones but aluminum is strong and light enough for virtually all uses. A very few tubes are made of steel. Recently, some tubes are using a magnesium alloy for added strength and a slightly lesser weight than aluminum but at an added cost.

From a structural standpoint, all of the materials are good. The wall thickness of any of the tube materials must be satisfactory to handle the rigorous functions of the riflescope.

Tube Finishes

The predominant tube finish today is a matte black. Why is this? It will come with a hard-anodized finish, which has virtually no reflections or glare. It is rugged, virtually scratchproof and immune to rust.

Courtesy of Bushnell

Courtesy of Nikon

You will also find glossy black, silver in matte or glossy, and some other colors. In many cases, the users are trying to match the color of their rifles, handguns, etc. and this is ok for target shooting. Nevertheless, for hunting purposes, shiny finishes are not good as they are subject to glare and reflections and are likely to scare off game.

You will also find camouflage models. Camouflage was more prevalent a decade ago and is less popular now. You will find inexpensive clamshell packed models in large retailers.

Courtesy of Truglo

A few manufacturers offer rubber covering on the tubes for a more rugged riflescope for use in extreme and unfriendly environments.

Reticles

Reticles are also called crosshairs, sighting references or graticules. Their main purpose is to allow hunters to place the aiming point within the riflescope on the animal or target. Reticle choice is very important and there are many considerations to make.

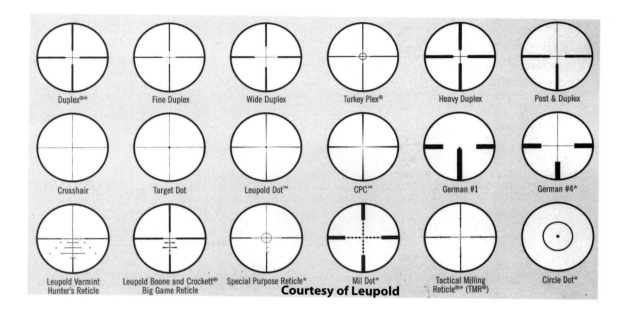

Courtesy of Leupold

Reticles come in a multitude of configurations and can be a system of posts (thick or thin), lines, bars, circles, dots, angles, numbers, etc. in your riflescope that appear superimposed on the target. Reticles range from a simple crosshair style, to plex styles, to very complex styles (Mil Dot, etc.) to allow hunters to estimate the distance to an animal or target (if the animal or target size is known), and to compensate for bullet drop (BDC) which may be difficult to use for some hunters.

Recommending a particular reticle type is difficult to do as the hunter has to take into consideration the type of hunting he will be doing and how easy he wants it to be – in other words, it comes down to personal choice.

Basic Crosshair Reticles

Up until the 1950s, the only reticle normally used was the basic crosshair. The crosshairs were made of spider web material or metal wire and put together very meticulously. These reticles are best for many small rodents, prairie dogs and varmints since usually the hunting distance is long and they only cover up a small amount of the target, which makes the target brighter and easy to see. They are also very good for target shooting.

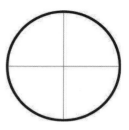

Plex Reticles

During the 1960s, the duplex reticle (still simple crosshairs with varying thickness of the lines and easy to use) was developed by Leupold & Stevens and became very popular. The duplex (and numerous similar or somewhat similar styles) are still very popular and are a great all-around choice for many hunters. Some manufacturers began using a photo-etching process on metal foil to make the reticles.

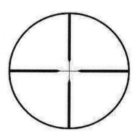

Courtesy of Bushnell

The plex (duplex, multiplex, and numerous other hybrids) typically have wide and thick crosshairs coming from the outer perimeter towards the center of the reticle. As the lines of the crosshairs near the center where they cross each other, the crosshairs become very narrow and fine allowing for accurate target placement. The thick crosshairs are easier to see in low light conditions or against busy backgrounds like forest or foliage. They are very good for big game hunting.

Some of the more complex designs allow for some range finding capability.

Both the basic crosshair reticle and plex type reticles are now mainly manufactured using thin etched glass. The etched glass style is stronger, more reliable and has the ability to provide complex designs easily. The negative to etched glass is that some of the light passing through the glass reticle is absorbed or lost to reflection. However, multi-coatings put on the glass minimize any absorption losses.

Mil-Dot Reticles

Put simply, using a set of fixed data references within a riflescope on the reticle, a hunter can compare sizes of the target (known object height) or a part of the target to the precision dots and spaces in order to calculate the true distance. These reticles have a series of dots coming from the center of the reticle on fine crosshairs.

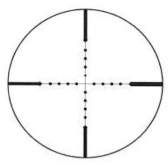

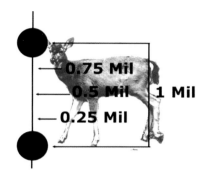

The "Mil" in Mil-Dot Reticle does not mean military (although the military extensively uses this type of reticle).

We use mils to find the distance to a target (where we know the height) which we need to know to aim the shot precisely. If we do not know the height of the target, then the reticle is useless.

Mil-Dot reticles calibrated at the factory are for only one magnification. In variable riflescopes, calibration is at the highest magnification.

Mil-Dot reticles are not for everyone (including me) as they take some time to understand and a lot of practice before they can be useful. Many people think they are too difficult to use, and they impair aiming due to the field of view "being cluttered" with dots, lines, circles, and numbers, etc. and this may be true. It takes time to calculate and is not the most accurate way to measure for distance. For those who do understand how to use them properly, they can be a big asset to the hunter and the military user for up to 1000 yards or meters.

The basic math may seem complex but bear with me. I have a hard time understanding and remembering this myself.

A Mil is $1/1000^{th}$ of a radian, or milliradian.

1 mil is 36 inches @ 1000 yards or 1 meter @ 1000 meters.

There are two basic types of Mil-Dots used throughout the world. There are actually additional ones used in the Soviet Union and in other countries but we will not discuss these here. Neither of the two basic types is better but they are just different.

The first one was (and continues to be) used by the U.S. Marine Corp where 6.2832 radians are in a circle. The math calculates out to 360/6.2832 = 57.3° per radian (6.2832 x 57.3 = 360° in a circle). Then, 6.2832 x 1000 = 6283.2 milliradians in a circle or 360/6283.2 = 0.0573°/milliradian (about $1/17^{th}$ of a degree or $1/6283^{rd}$ of a circle).

The second one is used by the U.S. Army (and most armies around the world use it), where 6400 milliradians are in a circle. The Army chose this method of radians using rounded numbers to make distance calculation easier for the users. The math calculates out to be 360/6.400 = 56.3° per radian (6.400 x 56.3 = 360° in a circle). Then, 6.400 x 1000 = 6400 milliradians in a circle or 360/6400 = 0.0563° milliradian ($1/6400^{th}$ of a circle).

The Marine style actually uses oblong dots rather than circular dots where the distance from the center of one dot to the center of the next dot equals 1 mil.

Basic formulas, that roughly obtain the target distances (they are not exact but references), were developed by the military but the same applies to hunting:

$$\frac{\text{Height of Target (yards or meters) x 1000}}{\text{Mils number (target height on reticle)}} = \text{Distance to Target - yards or meters}$$

Example – target is 2 yards (1.83 meters) high and is 5 mils on the reticle
2 x 1000/5 = 400 yards distance   or 1.83 x 1000/5 = 366 meters

For animals, the formula is easily changed to inches or centimeters:

$$\frac{\text{Height of Target (inches) x 27.78}}{\text{Mils number (target height on reticle)}} = \text{Distance to the Target in yards}$$

$$\frac{\text{Height of Target (centimeters) x 10}}{\text{Mils number (target height on reticle)}} = \text{Distance to the Target in meters}$$

Examples – whitetail deer height is 18 inches and is 1.25 mils on the reticle

18 x 27.78/1.25 = 400 yards distance

Using metric conversion of 400 yards into meters = 366 meters

Or the deer is 46 centimeters high and is 1.25 mils on the reticle

46x10/1.25 = 368 meters

Note: for animal height in the formula, use inches from the bottom of the brisket (breast or chest) to the top of the withers (ridge between the shoulder blades of a 4-legged animal). In the image here, see the circle for wither on top and brisket on bottom.

Typical height for a few animals:

Whitetail Deer 17–19 inches (43 –48cm)

Elk – 23 to 25 inches (58 to 66cm)

Bull Elk – 32 to 34 inches (81 to 86cm)

Pronghorn Antelope 14–16in.(36–41cm)

Caribou – 22 to 24 inches (56 to 61cm)

Coyote – 9 to 11 inches (23 to 28cm)

Sheep – 20 to 22 inches (51 to 56cm)

Courtesy of Bushnell

Rangefinding reticles are useful but using a laser rangefinder is much better, quicker and more accurate especially since there are so many choices now in the market.

Some hunters will use Mil-Dot reticles because they want a sophisticated item and the feeling of having a military style product. At the same time, manufacturers offer these reticles because demand is high for them.

Courtesy of Bruce Robinson

To take the difficulty out of the calculations and the time it consumes, there are alternatives. One company (Mildot Enterprises at www.mildot.com in the USA) offers an analog calculator designed along the principles of a slide rule to make the calculations for you quickly.

Personally, I prefer to use a laser rangefinder for distance measurements.

Mil-Dots and MOA

There is some confusion between Mils and MOA (Minutes of Angle/Arc). Reticles are marked using Mil-Dots, while adjustment through the turrets for wind and elevation, are made in fractions of a MOA (as discussed under adjustment controls for riflescopes). The difference is 1 mil = 3.438 MOA.

Both Mil-Dots and MOA are two common ways to measure angles for units of measure of a circle. Mil dots are much more useful and precise.

The relationship of Mils/MOA is expressed as:

$$\frac{3.438 \text{ min}}{1} \times \frac{1.047 \text{ inches}}{1 \text{ min}} = \frac{3.6}{\text{inches}} = 1 \text{ mil @ 100 yards}$$

Bullet Drop Compensation (BDC) Reticles

The main feature of bullet drop compensation (ballistic elevation) is the compensation for gravity on a bullet's trajectory at a given distance, which is "bullet drop".

You need to know or estimate the distance to your target.

Bullet trajectory and how it is affected by gravity is important, as a bullet fired from a rifle on an even plane will hit the ground at the same time a baseball will hit the ground when dropped by my hand. When I throw the baseball to a person 100 yards (91.4meters) away and the aim point is his glove, I will have to aim and throw much higher to compensate for gravity's effect or it will fall to the ground well before reaching him. How high I throw it, depends on the distance and speed I throw the ball.

Likewise, if I fire my rifle at a target 100 yards (91.4 meters) away when in a horizontal plane (with no bullet drop compensation), the bullet will land below center of the target.

BDC reticles usually have standard crosshairs or plex styles with small lines or circles on the vertical line below the center of the reticle, which is the amount of bullet drop over specific distances.

You make turret adjustments matched to your rifle, bullet caliber and weight, muzzle velocity and air density.

Note that with reticles focused on the second plane, they will work only at the magnification specified by the manufacturer whereas reticles focused on the first plane will work fine at any power.

More and more programs for BDC are available on manufacturer websites as well as smart phone apps.

In a perfect world, using BDC will allow your point of impact to be "spot on". However, assuming you correctly made the turret adjustments required above and you have the distance to the target exactly correct, there are many variables that you are faced with – batch number of the ammunition, temperature, humidity, elevation and many other factors. Any minor change can affect the aim in a big way and the further the distance the further off you may be.

Thus, BDC reticles will help you get close to your target. You can also get closer by knowing the exact distance to the target and a laser rangefinder will help you.

Reticle Positioning – Focal Plane

Riflescopes have two focal (image) planes. The first image plane is in front of the erecting lenses, closer to the objective lens where the image plane is upside down and reversed left to right. The other image plane is behind the erecting lenses, closer to the eyepiece where the image plane is right side up and correct left to right.

If you are using a fixed power riflescope, it is irrelevant which focal plane is used.

On all variable power riflescopes, it is important which image plane the reticle is located in.

The front image plane is the first focal plane (FFP) or objective image plane and the rear image plane is the second focal plane (SFP) or the eyepiece image plane. For example, the image plane shown below uses the first focal plane for the reticle location but you can see where the second focal plane is located when a riflescope uses this position for the reticle.

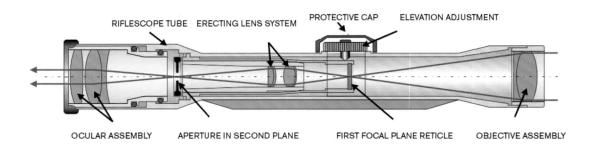

FFP reticle – will become larger or smaller depending on magnification changes, the same as the target. The advantage of this type of reticle placement is that when using range finding reticles (like Mil-Dots), they can be used at all magnifications with no problems. The disadvantage is that a reticle image may look great at low power but be cluttered and difficult to use at high power. Some reticles look sharp and good at high power but may be difficult to see at low power.

FFP reticles are European style (mainly because they can be very useful during night hunting in many European countries) although many Americans use them.

SFP reticle – will remain the same size when magnification changes but the target will become larger or smaller. The advantage of this type of reticle placement is that the reticle always has the same look and less cluttered at high magnifications. The main disadvantage is that when using range finding reticles (like Mil-Dots), they are only precise at one particular magnification set by the manufacturer – which is usually the highest power or up to 10x. A minor disadvantage is that the point of aim shifts ever so slightly during magnification changes as the lenses move tiny amounts during this process. However, many of the manufacturers now make the erecting image/power changing assembly more precise and sturdy, which eliminates any point of aim shifts.

SFP reticles are American style but many Europeans use this style also.

The two images at the top show the difference of the enlarged reticle and object (FFP) while the two images at the bottom show the difference of the enlarged object while the reticle size stays the same (SFP).

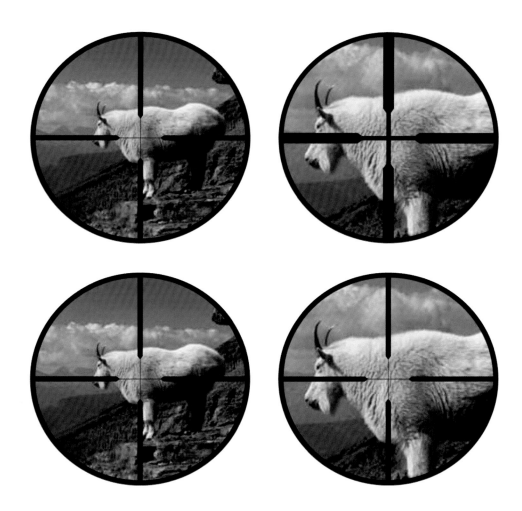

Background Image Courtesy of Bill McRae

Illuminated Reticles

Illuminated (lighted) reticles are popular with hunters (and military personnel) especially in low-light conditions as the reticles are much easier to see. They can even be helpful in full daylight for certain targets where the reticles stand out much more against thick foliage and forests.

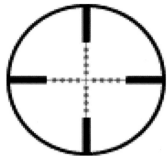

The illuminated reticles are generally battery operated using LEDs. Red color is the most common as it least impedes the shooters night vision (for Europeans hunting in darkness) in low light conditions. Various other colors can be better under certain conditions and many are switchable between different colors.

The illuminator should be variable in brightness (most are except some very low cost units) via built-in rheostats to adjust the reticle to the appropriate light available. On some low cost units, the minimum brightness is too bright and thus not useful.

These reticles add some weight and bulk to your riflescope.

The newest technology is electronically illuminated reticles. Radioactive isotopes (especially tritium elements), along with fiber optics, are seen more and more. Tritium illuminates the aiming point in low light conditions (beta rays from the tritium-hit phosphors to create the glow you see) without batteries and the fiber optics transmits the light. These new illuminating systems are more versatile than standard illumination systems.

Courtesy of Trijicon

Erector Tube Assembly

The erector tube assembly is part of a complete system that includes on most riflescopes the erector lenses, the reticle in some, springs, gimbals and many mechanical parts.

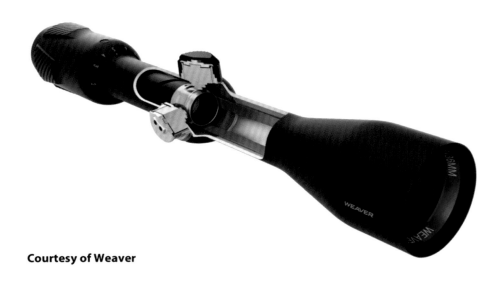

Courtesy of Weaver

All of the parts manufactured are to very precise tolerances to ensure a movement free mechanism that will hold precisely the point of impact while changing magnification and repeatedly do this over many years even withstanding the heavy recoil of many firearms.

The slight shifting of the point of impact (causing missed shots on the target) used to be more prevalent with second focal plane reticles. However, over the last ten years or so, the erector tube assemblies have become more reliable (with better materials, better machining to tighter tolerances and are more precisely assembled and tested to ensure repeated, accurate performance.

Parallax

Parallax is a problem with riflescopes due to the fact of the long eye relief associated with them as compared to binoculars and spotting scopes where the eye relief is relatively short and your eye(s) are up close to the eyepiece.

Parallax in optical riflescopes can be a problem. It can cause missed shots and a lot of frustration.

It results from the image formed by the objective lens not being coincident with the reticle (focused exactly on the reticle plane). In other words, the target shifts as you move your head at an angle to either side (left/right) or up and down from the center while looking through the eyepiece.

To demonstrate parallax, use your thumb and any finger to make a circle (or use a toilet paper tube). Then hold your hand (or the paper tube) at arm's length. Look through the circle at an object in a room or outside and then move your head slowly left or right and the object will move out of the circle. This is what parallax is.

Most riflescopes are parallax adjusted (parallax free) by the factory at a specific distance from 50 to 150 yards (46 to 137 meters) and at longer or shorter distances some parallax appears. At whatever specific distance, the focal plane of the target and the reticle is the same even if you look through the eyepiece at an angle to the optical axis.

Parallax is not a problem at all if your eye is in the center of the riflescopes optical axis regardless of power, exit pupil size, or distance to the target. A certain amount of parallax is present in virtually all riflescopes. However, if there is noticeable movement of the target it is not ok and will cause you problems.

Parallax cannot be corrected by adding compound lenses in the optical system, as the reticle does not move along the tube axis to provide any compensation. The target images at different distances fall at various points between the objective lens and the erector lenses and thus cause parallax.

Usually parallax is not a problem at low powers up to 6x or 9x (depending on the particular riflescope) due to large exit pupils. Most riflescopes of 10x or larger powers have some means of quick parallax adjustments the user can make – for a description of these controls see the section on Adjustment Controls.

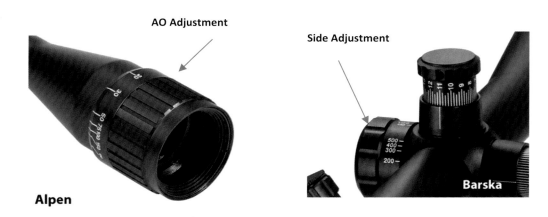

In riflescopes of low price and/or low quality, parallax can occur due to the reticle distance being positioned incorrectly from the objective lens, the reticle not being mounted securely, or a badly designed or manufactured objective lens.

Chapter 13 More Factors to Consider for Sport Optics

Waterproof Optical Products

True waterproof binoculars, spotting scopes and riflescopes are nitrogen (or argon) purged (filled) internally and O-ring sealed. The dry gas and purging prevent internal fogging from the elements, from altitude changes, from high humidity environments and from any small dots of moisture left mistakenly during the purging process at the factory.

Is there a difference between nitrogen and argon gas? Theoretically, argon purging should last a little longer than nitrogen due to its larger molecules, which do not leak as easily as smaller ones. The most important thing is not which inert gas you use but how good the seals are. Both nitrogen and argon gas are good and most of the commotion is from marketing departments. If you have some repair work done on your optical instrument and the firm has to purge it, most likely they only have the nitrogen gas to use.

Courtesy of Steiner

There are differing standards on waterproof specifications. Japan uses JIS7 (Japanese Industrial Standards) where units should withstand submersion in 1 meter (3.3 feet) of water for up to five minutes without leakage. This was the only specification used throughout the world in the 1980s and 1990s when the majority of binoculars and spotting scopes were made in Japan. The EU (and now much of the world) uses IEC (International Commission Publication) 60529 passed in 2002 which notes the IPX7 rating of submersion in 1 meter (3.3 feet) for 30 minutes. The IPX8 rating should be better than IPX7 but it has no actual specifications and leaves this up to each manufacturer, which does not make much sense.

Many optical products are labeled as waterproof but do not meet either the JIS or IEC ratings but can be submersible in water of less depth and time. They are nitrogen purged and truly waterproof. At the other end, some manufacturers have much better specifications than the standards and these are usually for military applications.

The interior of waterproof units are impervious to saltwater, moisture and dust. The nitrogen or argon gas prevents oxidation and internal fogging of the optical surfaces – thus, waterproof means also fogproof.

Waterproof optics are great for hunting, birding, boating and other wet weather activities.

Most riflescopes and the majority of binoculars (other than the lower cost models) and spotting scopes are waterproof. Most low-end sport optics products are not waterproof but many are water resistant (can handle some mist and light rain) and are fine in other than very wet conditions.

I recommend that you purchase only "true" waterproof products that are nitrogen or argon purged and you will not be sorry.

I laugh at all the various terms manufacturers use for water-resistant — they are not waterproof but they lead you to believe they are. Here is a sampling; moisture resistant, splashproof, sprayproof, fogproof, rainproof, weatherproof and finally showerproof.

Waterproof Testing
Image Courtesy of Leupold & Stevens, Inc.

Thermal Shock/Exposure Test
Image Courtesy of Leupold & Stevens, Inc.

There are ways to test a riflescope, binocular, and spotting scope that is supposed to be waterproof. Do these at your own risk, as not all manufacturers will take the product back as being defective knowing how you did the tests.

Immerse the optic in warm water, 12" to 18" (30 to 46 cm) deep for a few minutes (makes the nitrogen gas expand) and watch for any bubbles and if bubbles appear the product may be defective. Then, make sure the instrument is dry and at room temperature. Then, put it in a freezer for a few hours to see if there is any internal fogging up or bubbles appear and if so the product may be defective.

Another way is to reverse the process above and put the product in a freezer for a few hours. Then, take it out and immerse in warm water, 12" to 18" (30 to 46 cm) deep, for a few minutes to check for any bubbles or internal fogging that may appear.

The above tests are extremely rough on the optics and you may not encounter the same conditions in the field. You may encounter briefly some external fogging but do not worry about this.

Warranty

Binoculars, spotting scopes, and riflescopes having a long warranty is important to many people especially if you purchase a medium or high priced unit. In reality, major defects or flaws in most optical products are discovered immediately after you purchase them or in the first few years. Warranties that are at least two years or more should leave most people secure about their purchase.

There are required warranty time limits in the EU whereas in the U.S.A. there is no specified time requirements but the Federal Trade Commission rules call out what the manufacturers must say.

Investigate the warranty prior to purchase as just a title (lifetime warranty or however many years) may mean different things from different manufacturers. Full details should be available to see on the website of any brand and if no details are available then that should be a sign of caution, as you are not sure what you are going to get. Most manufacturers will back up their products. An example of an excellent warranty is below and keep in mind that there are many good warranties available from other manufacturers.

Our warranty is about you, not us. It's about taking care of you after the sale. The VIP stands for a **V**ery **I**mportant **P**romise to you, our customers. We will repair or replace your Vortex product in the event it becomes damaged or defective—at no charge to you. It doesn't matter how it happened, whose fault it was, or where you purchased it. You can count on the VIP Warranty for all **riflescopes**, **red dots**, **rangefinders**, **binoculars**, **spotting scopes** and **monoculars**.

- Unlimited Lifetime Warranty
- Fully transferable
- No warranty card to fill out
- No receipt needed to hang on to

If you ever have a problem, no matter the cause, we promise to take care of you. The VIP warranty does not cover loss, theft or deliberate damage to the product...that's it.

Chapter 14   Final Items for Decision Making

Binoculars

Body Covering — this is a very subjective area. Most binoculars come with a rubber type covering. Hunters normally demand rubber covering. The rubber withstands shock and rough handling and protects your binocular. The rubber can be very thin or rather thick. Other binoculars come with a leatherette type finish, some have an anodized aluminum finish and others have various materials and styles.

Courtesy of Truglo   **10x42**

The body finishes can be of many different colors with the predominant color in the market being black with green the next most popular color. The look and feel of the binocular to you is most important, as this is a personal decision of your choice.

Case — most binoculars come with a case. Generally, as the price of the product goes up, the style of case, construction and protection is better. When not using your binoculars, it is best to keep them in the case to keep them clean and protected.

Compass — some binoculars come with compasses to find your location. They are useful for boaters, hunters, surveillance, land viewing, etc.

Minox

Comfort — the ease of holding a binocular for long periods should be a consideration. Whether you are considering a Porro prism or roof prism design, it is important that you feel comfortable holding them.

Construction — the security of the barrel alignment and the internal mounting of the optics are important to a long binocular life, free of user eye fatigue. It is difficult for you to determine how well a binocular is constructed but again, price is your best guideline – in general, the higher the price, the better the construction.

The open bridge (hinge) design has become more popular in several mid and high-end models. The open bridge (uses two small hinges near the focus knob and the objective lenses) has a gap between the hinges that lets your fingers fit around the tube barrels where you can comfortably use the binocular with one hand (although much depends on the size of your hand and space available). The standard bridge (closed) design uses one large hinge. Personally, I prefer the open bridge design as most that I have used have allowed me to use one hand and I like this.

Courtesy of Celestron

Courtesy of Carson Optical

Open Bridge design above left and Standard Bridge Design above right

Binoculars can have the main body made of plastic material or metal (usually aluminum) and either can work well. On several mid and higher-end products, you will find magnesium alloy used which is more rugged and lighter in weight.

It is helpful to have most of the internal parts, including the main tubes, to have their finish be as "optically flat black" as possible to eliminate or minimize glare and reflections, which can affect the overall optical image.

Filters and Sunshades — they are mounted in various ways (fitting over or clipped onto the objective lenses, over the eyepieces, threaded in the objective or eyepiece lenses, etc.) for specialized uses.

Filter and Sunshade styles and types come on and off the market but the more prevalent ones (when offered) are the following:

> *Solar* — allows you to observe safely the Sun for fantastic views of sunspots and granules with properly designed solar filters. The filters are of glass or Mylar film. The most important thing is to make sure the filter attaches securely to the binocular to ensure your safety.

#12 Yellow — generally improves visibility through haze and over water especially in low light and cloudy days. Resolution and contrast is improved.

Polarizing — cuts down on glare in bright light conditions.

Sunshades – these reduce glare and bright reflections from the Sun and other bright objects. It is easier to see objects and does not scare off wildlife who can become frightened when they see reflections off binocular glass.

Courtesy of Carson Optical

Harness – an accessory that you wear that is very useful for hunters, birders and other outdoor users.

Compared to the conventional neck strap of binoculars, the binocular harness takes the strain off your neck and distributes the weight load to your shoulders and torso.

Courtesy of Swarovski

Courtesy of Bushnell

It is very comfortable to wear and in addition safely keeps the binoculars close to you when carrying them during extended hours in the field.

Objective Lens and Eyepiece Caps — most binoculars come with caps to prevent dust and other contaminants from accumulating on the optical elements when not in use. On some high-end binoculars, caps are accessories.

The quality of most caps has improved over the years. Many mid and high end objective lens caps now are conveniently semi-attached or permanently attached to the binocular, to prevent them from becoming easily lost. The eyepiece caps on most mid and high-end binoculars are a one-piece design (called a rain guard) that fits over both eyepieces to prevent losing two small traditional type caps.

Reticles — a ranging scale (reticle) helps in determining the distance you are from objects. These are good for boaters, hunters, military personnel, etc.

Smart Phone Adapters – during the last year, there has appeared in the market several different adapters to adapt your smart phone to a binocular.

Some adapters are made for specific phones and others are universal types than fit most smart phones.

These designs make it quite easy to view and or take images through your

Courtesy of Carson Optical

binocular. What you see on the phone screen is the object with the magnification of the binocular.

You can take snapshots or videos to expand the use of your binocular and hobby.

Straps — most binoculars come with a thin neck strap. As the binocular price goes up, many models are supplied with a wider cloth (or other material) strap which is more comfortable and much easier on your neck. If you have a very thin neck strap, consider buying an optional, higher quality strap.

Tripod Adaptability — most full size binoculars have threads (1/4 x 20) in order to attach a binocular tripod adapter that allows you to mount the binoculars on a photographic/video tripod for more stable, vibration-free viewing. Be sure to use a stable tripod or you will not achieve the purpose of using a tripod — stability!

To mount this adapter, remove the hinge cap, thread the adapter screw into the hinge socket and tighten. The other end of the adapter mounts to the pan head of the tripod.

Weight – can be important especially during long hours when you are in the field. Every ounce (gram) can burden you and thus unnecessary, extra weight is to be avoided. There are benefits to larger objective lenses but they add weight and consider this when making your product choices. Try to compare various models you are considering as even the same power and objective lens size can vary considerably in weight and size in different brands depending on the design and materials used.

Window Mount – expand the use of your binoculars by turning most any vehicle into a viewing and or imaging platform.

You use the window mount on any window that is convenient for you to view or image from.

Courtesy of Kenko

Spotting Scopes

Body Covering — this is a very subjective area. Most spotting scopes come with a rubber covering or a rubberized paint. Hunters normally demand this. The rubber withstands shock and rough handling and protects your binocular. The rubber can be very thin or rather thick. Other spotting scopes come with a painted finish, anodized aluminum finish, etc.

Case — many spotting scopes come with a case. Generally, as the price of the product goes up, the style of case, construction and protection is better. When not using your spotting scope, it is best to keep it in the case to keep it clean. Better cases are "stay on" types as you use the spotting scope without entirely removing it from the case.

Construction — the internal mounting of the optics is important to a long spotting scope life, free of user eye fatigue. It is difficult for you to determine how well a spotting scope is constructed but again, price is your best guideline; in general, the higher the price, the better the construction.

Spotting scopes may have the main body made of plastic material or metal (usually aluminum) and either can work well. On some higher-end products, you will find magnesium alloy used which is more rugged and lighter in weight.

Over the last decade or so, a much higher percentage of spotting scopes have a rubber or armored coating or paint on the main body or more of the instrument to prevent against damage in the field and this is a good idea.

It is helpful to have most of the internal parts, including the main tube, to have their finish be as "optically flat black" as possible to eliminate or minimize glare and reflections that can affect the overall optical image.

Digiscoping Adaptors – so much enjoyment can be experienced with taking images through your spotting scope. There are various ways of taking images described earlier in the book but I feel it is important to emphasize it again here.

There are many ways to take images through your spotting scope and each brand and/or model may do it differently and you will have to see how to do this by looking at your instruction manual. Most of the attachments are optional items but some may be included with certain brands and models.

Taking images through spotting scopes has become quite popular and the common term for this activity is "digiscoping". There are a few ways of doing this:

1. Using a point and shoot digital camera. You can hold your digital camera centered directly behind the eyepiece of the spotting scope and take images. This is not the easiest way to do it, as obtaining focus and holding your camera steady can create problems as you are shooting at high powers. I tried this a few years back a couple of times and did obtain some decent shots but only after a lot of frustration.

The most common way is to use a dedicated or universal digital camera adapter. The adapter will have adjustment controls in both axes, in and out so that you can center and focus the object easily prior to taking images. Make sure you follow the manufacturer's instructions.

Courtesy of Celestron

2. Using a SLR or DSLR camera. With this method, you will attach your camera to an adapter in one of several different ways, depending on the spotting scope type you have.

Becoming more popular in digiscoping, is the use of pancake lenses (with a dedicated adapter) for projection imaging.

Some brands use T-Adapters that thread onto the spotting scope (in various ways) and you then need a T-Ring for your particular brand of camera (after removing the camera lens) that adapts to your T-Adapter. Some brands have built-in T-Adapter threads, which you then adapt a T-Ring for your particular camera brand.

Courtesy of Leica

3. Smart phones attach to many spotting scopes and adapters are available from many companies. It is simple to take images and share views on your phone.

Some adapters are made for specific phones and others are universal types than fit most smart phones.

These adapters make it easy to view and take images through your spotting scope. What you see on the phone screen is the object with the magnification of the spotting scope.

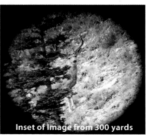

You can take snapshots or videos to expand the use of your spotting scope. This is quite enjoyable as it expands your hobby.

There are numerous articles and lots of information online about digiscoping and I suggest you read as much as possible. There are many techniques and tips available you can use to maximize the quality of your images.

Eyepiece Position – as described briefly earlier, whether you look through the eyepiece in a straight line relative to the main body and objective lens (straight through spotting scope) or at a 45° position (angled spotting scope) is a personal preference.

The angled type is the most popular for a number of reasons such as – easier to use when sharing the spotting scope and people are of different heights as you only set the tripod for comfortable use by the shortest person, allows you to aim skyward to see eagles or hawks flying above or birds high up in a tree. The angled style may be harder to aim at first but will become easier once you are familiar with it. For myself, I prefer the straight types most of the time as I like aiming the eyepiece while I am aligning down the main tube and this is easier for me but it can be rough on your neck when looking up at things and raising the tripod may take too long, etc.

Filters and Sunshades — attach in various ways (fitting or clipping over the objective lens, over the eyepiece, threaded in the objective or eyepiece lens, etc.) for specialized uses. Many spotting scopes have sliding self-storing sunshades.

Filter and Sunshade styles and types come on and off the market but the more prevalent ones (when offered) are the following:

Solar — they allow you to observe the Sun in a safe manor, for fantastic views of sunspots and granules with properly designed solar filters. The filters can be made of glass or Mylar film. The most important thing is to make sure the filter attaches securely to the spotting scope to ensure your safety.

#12 Yellow — generally improves the visibility through haze and over water especially in low light and on cloudy days. Resolution and contrast is improved.

Polarizing — cuts down on glare in bright light conditions.

Sunshades – these reduce glare and bright reflections from the Sun and other bright objects. It is easier to see objects and does not scare off wildlife who can become frightened when they see reflections off the spotting scope objective lens.

Objective Lens and Eyepiece Caps — most spotting scopes come with caps to prevent dust and other contaminants from accumulating on the optical elements when not in use. On some high-end spotting scopes, they are accessories.

In recent years, the caps offered on many mid and high-end products are more rugged, durable and harder to lose.

Tripod — make sure to use a stable and rigid tripod to mount your spotting scope on or you will not achieve the purpose of using a tripod — stability!

Courtesy
of Zeiss

Weight – can be important especially during long hours when you are in the field. Every ounce (gram) can burden you and thus unnecessary, extra weight is to be avoided if possible. There are benefits to larger objective lenses but they add weight and consider this when making your product choices. Try to compare various models you are considering as even the same power and objective lens size can vary considerably in weight and size in different brands depending on the design and materials used.

Window Mount – expand the use of your spotting scope by turning most any vehicle into a viewing and or imaging platform.

You use the window mount on any window that is convenient for you to view or image from.

Courtesy of Kenko

Riflescopes

Action/Helmet Cameras – several brands are adaptable with a riflescope to video your hunting experience so you can review it later or share with your friends. Higher end versions offer Wi-Fi capability so you can stream your video live, assuming you have the proper connections available.

Courtesy of Midland Radio

Anemometers (Wind Gauges) – are a handy aid to hunters and target shooters. They measure basic wind speed. Other features included on higher cost units are average speed, maximum speed, wind gusts, temperature, wind chill, barometer, hygrometer and altimeter.

Courtesy of Celestron

Construction – riflescopes must endure extreme environmental conditions (temperature, humidity, rain, snow and many other things), heavy recoil from firearms and rough handling, etc. Typically most mid and high priced riflescopes are precision manufactured and should not have problems. Most problems arise in lower priced units where the factories use less expensive materials, less precise machining, do less quality control tests, etc. and thus have more problems.

A properly manufactured riflescope should be durable and repeatable and assumed that the optics and other components will perform as expected.

It is helpful to have most of the internal parts, including the main tube, to have their finish be as "optically flat black" as possible to eliminate or minimize glare and reflections that can affect the overall optical image.

Filters and Sunshades — mount in various ways (fitting or clipping over the objective lens, over the eyepiece, threaded into the objective housing, etc.) for specialized uses.

Filters were more prevalent a decade or more ago, and very few currently and if they were available, the most useful would be:
> _#12 Yellow_ — improves the visibility through haze and over water especially in low light and on cloudy days. Resolution and contrast will be improved.
> _Polarizing_ — cuts down on glare in bright light conditions.

Sunshades sell as an accessory, but are included with some models. They reduce glare and bright reflections from the Sun and other bright objects.

Currently a few brands are offering a specialized lens shade that fits over the objective lens that uses a honeycomb structure which makes it easier to find your target. It also does not scare game away due to reflections off the objective lens. It also protects the objective lens from scratches and other hazards. However, there will be some minor light loss due to the obstruction from the honeycomb.

GPS Handheld Devices – Entry-level units are handy devices to prevent you from getting lost out in the field. Units that are more expensive allow you to keep track of your travels through trail and data point collection and may allow for uploading on Google Maps or other sites. Many other features are available on different models.

Mounting System – the mounting system for riflescopes to a firearm (rifle, shotgun, or pistol) is an important decision and almost as important as your choice of riflescope because even the finest riflescope with a great firearm will do you no good if the riflescope is not mounted to the firearm properly.

The mounting system consists of rings that hold the riflescope in place and are mounted to the bases that hold the rings and riflescope to the firearm securely.

Several riflescope manufacturers offer their own mounting systems but there is an abundance of standardized systems available in the marketplace. Some of the more popular mounting systems include B-Square, Burris, DNZ, Kwik-Site, Leapers, Leupold, Millett, Redfield, S & K, Talley, Warne, and Weaver.

If you mount your riflescope yourself, make sure you follow the manufacturers' torque specifications for both the base and rings.

Just remember, do not skimp on price as the mounting system is important and you want to have a rugged, reliable and satisfactory experience each time you hunt or target shoot.

Objective Lens and Eyepiece Lens Caps (Covers) — these help to prevent dust and other contaminants from accumulating on the optical elements when not in use or out in the field during bad weather. They normally are included with the riflescope. However, some are as accessories and they come in different configurations – slide over, clip over, flip up/down, screw in, etc. Some are made of a transparent material.

Rangefinders – the most common, laser rangefinders, are a handy item to use when hunting as it makes judging distances a snap.

They are useful in a variety of other activities when knowing the distance is important or if you just want to know what the object is.

Courtesy of Vortex Optics

They have been around since the mid-1960s but have continued to evolve with better technology along with lower pricing.

Courtesy of Bushnell

Courtesy of Zeiss

Courtesy of Zeiss

Most laser rangefinders are with monocular vision but binocular vision is available.

The lower cost units typically range to 400 yards (366 meters) and higher costs units range up to 1000 to 2000 yards (900 to 1800 meters).

Shooting Glasses – they are for your eye protection. I would suggest you use shooting glasses whether for sport hunting or target shooting. There are many hazards such as flying debris and other airborne hazards that can damage your eyes and you need protection from "blow-back" and "bounce-back".

Courtesy of Randolph

In addition to eye protection, good shooting glasses can improve your aim. With colored/tinted lenses, they can help you see better in different conditions – bright glare, low light, etc. The more common colors are clear for indoor shooting, yellow, gray and magenta for cutting down glare and increasing contrast and polarizing for cutting haze and glare. There are many other colors available for different conditions and some brands offer interchangeable lens colors as a kit.

The most popular and strongest lenses are made of polycarbonate, which are also very light in weight. Polycarbonate also offers protection from UVA-UVB light.

There are many, many brands and models to choose from in the market. For shooting glasses, due to fashion costs,

Courtesy of Randolph

you cannot in general say that the best protection is at the highest cost.

You should consider the amount of protection and at least get those that have ANSI Z87.1 certification and even more protection if certified to MIL-PRF-31013. In addition, comfort and fit are important as well.

Smart Phone Adapters – during the last year, several adapters have appeared in the market to hook your smart phone to a riflescope.

These designs make it quite easy to view and or take images through your riflescope. What you see on the phone LCD screen is the object with the magnification of the riflescope.

You can take snapshots or video to record your hunting experiences.

Courtesy of theiScope

Courtesy of theiScope

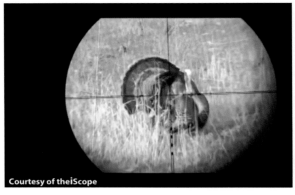

Courtesy of theiScope

Courtesy of theiScope

Weight – is extremely important especially during long hunting trips when you are in the field for hours. Every extra ounce (gram) can burden you and extra weight should be avoided, if possible. There are benefits to larger objective lenses, larger main tubes, illuminators, etc. but they all add weight and consider this when making your product choices.

Chapter 15   Inspection, Storing, Cleaning and Repair

Initial Inspection

When you first buy a pair of binoculars, spotting
scope, or riflescope, check the overall appearance.
Make sure the outside of the unit is clean and free
of scratches or dents.

Courtesy of Celestron

Check the optical appearance (objective lenses,
eyepieces, prisms and coatings) for any scratches,
dirt or other obvious defects both on the exterior and on the interior. Note that if looking
into the interior with a flashlight through the objective or eyepiece ends, you may see
very, very slight scratches on the glass surfaces and just ignore them as it is due to the light
beam of the flashlight and not a good optical test method.

Inspect the focusing mechanism for smoothness.

Then look through the optics at an object to check optical quality (be sure to adjust the
diopter for binoculars first). You should be able to focus sharply and feel no eye
discomfort. Do not look through windows and expect the same sharpness as you would
outdoors. Many windows are made of poor
optical glass that is especially noticeable when
you are looking out at an angle.

To verify optical quality there are a few things
you can do. Testing can verify any severe
aberrations.

Courtesy of Kenko

Look at a building or wall or other object that has straight lines and fills the entire field of
view – check the straightness of the lines from the center to the edge of the field. Then
check for sharpness at the center and the edge.

Now look at a sign, chart or decorative building outside in daylight that is bright.   Check
for sharpness, brightness and natural colors. Try to be at least 25 yards (meters) away
from the target at the lowest power and then increase the power (if a zoom).

You can look at a chart or other object with fine detail in the darkened corner of a store or an object outside at twilight to ascertain the brightness and detail available. The image for about 65% to 75% of the central part of the field should give very sharp images free of most color aberration. With most optical products (except higher end products), the outer part of the field of view and especially the edges will have aberrations such as distortion, field curvature and especially chromatic aberration all of which is normal.

6-24x56   **Courtesy of Zeiss**

Binoculars, spotting scopes and riflescopes do not need routine maintenance other than making sure the objectives and eyepieces are clean. If repairs become necessary, the manufacturer or a qualified repair company should service them.

As noted earlier in this book, collimation is the biggest concern with binoculars. If your binoculars are roughly handled, or dropped, there is a good chance that the collimation will be "out". If so, you need to have your binoculars serviced so that you can enjoy your product.

Storing and Caring for Optical Products

Your product is a precision optical instrument, and it should be treated with care. It should last you many years with little or no maintenance if you keep it clean and stored properly.

Do not drop your product if possible or it may become damaged. Do not leave your instrument in a vehicle on a hot day, if possible, as this could cause damage. Do not expose your instrument to water or moisture unless it is waterproof.

When not using your instrument, please keep any caps or covers in place. Keep it in a case, if available, to keep dust and other contaminants off.

Store your instrument in a cool, dry and clean place. If your product had a small bag of desiccant (silica gel), please place it close to the product, as it will help prevent moisture from the surrounding environment. Even if your product is waterproof, the exterior can still be susceptible to moisture and other contaminants.

Cleaning Optical Surfaces

Most people do not consider to clean their optics and this can harm the optical performance. Dirty objective lenses and/or eyepieces mean less light transmission and loss of brightness as well as un-sharp images. Keep your optics clean to enjoy the best that they can offer you! Really dirty and grimy objective lens and eyepiece lens surfaces can cause a light loss of 25% to 50%.

At the same time, do not over clean too often just to remove a piece of dust, etc. as excessive cleaning can easily damage the coatings on your optics.

The outer surfaces of the lenses are what you have to be concerned with most. Fingerprints, dust, dirt, smudges, oil and other contaminants

Courtesy of Swarovski

are all things to be of concern. Keep your optics clean!

Avoid touching the glass surfaces but if fingerprints (which can contain mild acid) get on them, clean as soon as possible to avoid damaging the optical coatings.

To clean the optical surfaces, I recommend a lens/optics cleaning kit available at most optical suppliers and many specialty sporting goods retailers. If you have multi-coatings there are special cleaning kits especially made for these. If you have a lot of dust or dirt accumulated, brush it off gently with a camel's hair brush and/or utilize a can of pressurized air. Then use the cleaning kit.

A number of manufacturers offer optical cleaning kits. There are also cleaning tools such as the Lenspen® that works well to keep your optics clean.

Courtesy of Celestron

 It is useful to have micro-fiber cleaning cloths available to help you keep your optics clean.

If you do not have access to the above, you can clean your optics with acetone and use **white** tissues (do not used colored or scented tissues). Put the acetone on the tissue and then use the tissue on the glass and rub in straight lines (do not rub in circles) from the center out to the edge for best results. When using acetone, please ensure your work area is well ventilated. You can also use isopropyl alcohol for cleaning.

Whatever cleaning kits or tools you use, please follow the manufacturers' instructions in order to do the best job and avoid scratching the fragile coatings or the lenses.

Note: Never clean optical surfaces with cloth or paper towels as they can easily scratch optical surfaces.

Repair

If at any time, your optical instrument needs repair work, do not attempt to perform this yourself. Most major things that go wrong with your product probably are covered by your warranty.

Please contact the manufacturer for warranty items and if the problems are not covered, the manufacturer should be able to repair it a reasonable cost.

If your product is not covered by a warranty, and the manufacturer cannot or will not repair it, then contact a qualified repair company to do the work.

Chapter 16   Who Manufactures Optical Products?

Virtually all **binoculars** sold in the U.S.A. are imported and thus it is easier to project what the market size is. The vast majority of binoculars (92.9% of all units imported to the U.S.A.) are manufactured in China. In dollar amounts imported, China accounts for 53.6% and the combined imports from Japan, Austria and Germany account for

Courtesy of Zeiss

34.2%. In past decades, the medium and high-end products mainly come from Japan, Germany and Austria. However, in the last decade, many Chinese factories have manufactured medium priced binoculars and a few are now making higher-end products and are close in quality to the Japanese and European products. Binoculars are imported duty free into the U.S.A.

Courtesy of Celestron

Spotting scopes are harder to determine just how many units and the dollar amount is imported. This is because many importers use various HTS (Harmonized Tariff Schedule) codes. There is a specific code for spotting scopes (import tariff is 6.6%) but many companies include them under the astronomical telescope or other codes. However, where they are imported from, in my opinion, is very similar to binoculars. As with binoculars, the Chinese factories are producing higher and higher quality in spotting scopes. Similar to binoculars, virtually all spotting scopes sold in the U.S.A. are imported.

Riflescopes are similar to binoculars in that they are mainly imported under one HTS code and figuring out the imported units and dollar value is relatively easy to calculate. For units imported over the last twenty years, China has dominated this category and accounted for 71.6% of imports last year. Likewise, China has been the leader for the same period for dollar value of riflescopes imported until this past year when the Philippines surpassed China (32.6%) with 34.0% of the dollar value of imports and part of the reason is that imports from the Philippines is duty free. In dollar value of imports, the combined value combined from Japan, Austria and Germany accounts for 26.1%.

However, calculating the market size is somewhat more difficult than the other categories because there are many riflescopes manufactured in the U.S.A. I estimate that 40% of all riflescopes sold in the U.S.A. were not imported although some components were. They have some level of manufacturing done in the U.S.A. Many companies assemble and test in the U.S.A., several manufacture some components and a few manufacture most of the riflescope.

I am skeptical that any riflescope is 100% American made as undoubtedly some

components are imported as I have seen various component parts for several brands designated for shipment to the U.S.A. in various factories in Asia.

There are a number of reasons that the manufacturing percentage of riflescopes in the U.S.A is relatively high. First, some military purchases

Courtesy of Vortex Optics

require a certain percentage of the products value to be produced in the U.S.A. Then, some (especially higher-end) products are assembled and tested in the U.S.A. to avoid the high import duty (14.9% currently on optical riflescopes except for certain countries like South Korea and the Philippines which have no import tax) and they import the various components which alone have a low import duty rate.

The latest import statistics available for the U.S.A. are for the complete 2012 year. The U.S. Department of Commerce and the U.S. International Trade Commission compile the data. Detailed historical information of imports for binoculars and riflescopes are in the Appendices to this book.

I will comment briefly on factories producing optical products. I have been to China 40 or more times and to Japan 20 or more times as well as to other countries visiting factories and have lost count of how many total factories I have seen in the optical and electronics industries. Contrary to what the media in the U.S.A. would have everyone believe, factories in China are quite modern and over the years, they have improved immensely the working environment, conditions, wages, etc. The productivity in Chinese factories is very high and the workers have a desire to produce high quality products. The Japanese and European factories are very nice and I am always impressed with the workers and the product quality.

Chapter 17   What New Technology Will Be Coming?

I do not expect many revolutionary products in the next few years but a continuation of evolutionary products. Below are some of the things that I expect to happen:

- Better quality optical components such as new developments in low dispersion glass or elements, which would be superior to what is currently available but lower in cost for objective lenses, a higher density glass than BaK-4 but at a reasonable price for prisms and better quality glass and designs for eyepieces.
- Higher performance optical coatings with the ultimate in coating design along with the elimination of internal reflections and glare to achieve the finest possible throughput transmission at no increase in cost.
- Lower cost for magnesium alloy bodies or a new type of material with similar characteristics to lower weight and increase strength.
- New Image stabilized binoculars at a more reasonable cost than is available today. New technology hopefully that will be developed that keeps the weight low.
- Image stabilization built into riflescopes to assist in accuracy of shooting.
- Laser rangefinders built in to binoculars and riflescopes at a modest cost
- Filters that easily attach to binoculars, spotting scopes and riflescopes that aid observing under various environmental conditions.
- Red dot or similar technology, built into spotting scopes for easy alignment.
- More user friendly and low cost GPS technology with digital compasses built in to binoculars, spotting scopes and riflescopes.
- Development of apps for smart phones that allow more enjoyment out of sport optics hobbies, like bird watching, hunting, astronomy and other activities.
- New software that is more user-friendly and built into binoculars and spotting scopes for easy bird identification.
- Higher quality optical components and designs to enable the use of higher power eyepieces for spotting scopes at target ranges, for birding and for spotting game that provide steady and brilliant views.
- Introduction of newer and more user-friendly body styles for binoculars and spotting scopes that look "cool" and have all the components and outer housings being environmentally friendly.
- New computerized riflescope designs and/or software with "heads-up" LCDs that take the human error out of aiming, all at a cost than many sport hunters can afford.
- Development of secure optical, voice and data communications with sets of binoculars or spotting scopes with line of site up to 2 miles (3.2 km) or more.
- I hope that some new revolutionary ideas will turn into sport optics products in the near future, which will be great for any hobby you have.

Appendix A   Metric and English Conversion

mm	in	ft	yd	cm	in	ft	m	ft	yd	km	mile
1	0.04	0.00	0.00	1	0.39	0.03	1	3.28	1.09	1	0.62
10	0.39	0.03	0.01	10	3.94	0.33	2	6.56	2.19	10	6.21
20	0.79	0.07	0.02	20	7.87	0.66	3	9.84	3.28	60	37.28
30	1.18	0.10	0.03	30	11.81	0.98	10	32.81	10.94	100	62.14
40	1.57	0.13	0.04	40	15.75	1.31	100	328.08	109.36		
100	3.94	0.33	0.11	100	39.37	3.28	200	656.17	218.72		
500	19.69	1.64	0.55	500	196.85	16.40	300	984.25	328.08		
1000	39.37	3.28	1.09	1000	393.70	32.81	400	1,312.34	437.45		
							500	1,640.42	546.81		
							1000	3,280.84	1,093.61		

mm (millimeters) x 0.03937 = inches
cm (centimeters) x 0.39370 = inches
m (meters) x 1.09361 = yards
km (kilometers) x 0.62137 = miles

in	mm	cm	m	ft	cm	m	yd	m	mile	km
0.5	12.70	1.27	0.01	1	30.00	0.30	1	0.91	1	1.61
1	25.40	2.54	0.03	2	61.00	0.61	10	9.14	10	16.09
2	50.80	5.08	0.05	3	91.00	0.91	50	45.72	60	96.56
3	76.20	7.62	0.08	10	304.80	3.05	100	91.44	100	160.93
4	101.60	10.16	0.10	20	609.60	6.10	200	182.88		
10	254.00	25.40	0.25	50	1,524.00	15.24	300	274.32		
50	1,270.00	127.00	1.27	100	3,048.00	30.48	400	365.76		
							500	457.20		
							1000	914.40		

in (inch) x 25.4000 = mm
ft (feet) x 30.4800 = cm
yd (yard) x 0.91440 = m
m (mile) x 1.60934 = km

g	oz	p	kg	oz	p	oz	g	p	kg
1	0.04	0.00	1	35.27	2.20	1	28.35	1	0.45
10	0.35	0.02	2	70.55	4.41	2	56.70	2	0.91
30	1.06	0.07	5	176.37	11.02	5	141.75	5	2.27
100	3.53	0.22	10	352.74	22.05	10	283.50	10	4.54
500	17.64	1.10	25	881.85	55.12	25	708.74	25	11.34
1000	35.27	2.20							

g (gram) x 0.0353 = ounces   oz (ounce) x 28.350 = grams
kg (kilogram) x 2.2046 = pounds   p (pounds) x 0.4536 = kilograms

Appendix B   Exit Pupil (EP) Size of Optical Instruments

Size	EP		Size	EP		Size	EP
5x15	3.0		16x25	1.6		8x33	4.1
6x16	2.7		17x25	1.5		9x33	3.7
7x18	2.6		20x25	1.3		6x35	5.8
1x20	20.0		21x25	1.2		7x35	5.0
2x20	10.0		27x25	0.9		8x35	4.4
3x20	6.7		28x25	0.9		9x35	3.9
4x20	5.0		80x25	0.3		10x35	5.5
5x20	4.0		7x26	3.7		12x35	2.9
6x20	3.3		8x26	3.3		15x35	2.3
7x20	2.9		8.5x26	3.1		17x35	2.1
8x20	2.5		10x26	2.6		20x35	1.8
9x20	2.2		9x27	3.0		6x36	6.0
10x20	2.0		10x27	2.7		7x36	5.1
5x21	4.2		8x28	3.5		8x36	4.5
6x21	3.5		9x28	3.1		10x36	3.6
6.5x21	3.2		10x28	2.8		12x36	3.0
7x21	3.0		10.5x28	2.7		3x40	13.3
8x21	2.6		4x30	7.5		4x40	10.0
8.5x21	2.5		6x30	5.0		6x40	6.7
10x21	2.1		7x30	4.3		7x40	5.7
8x22	2.8		8x30	3.8		8x40	5.0
6x23	3.8		9x30	3.3		9x40	4.4
8x23	2.9		10x30	3.0		10x40	4.0
10x23	2.3		12x30	2.5		12x40	3.3
12x23	1.9		1x32	32.0		14x40	2.9
1x24	24.0		2x32	16.0		15x40	2.7
4x24	6.0		3x32	10.7		16x40	2.5
6x24	4.0		4x32	8.0		18x40	2.2
7x24	3.4		5x32	6.4		21x40	1.9
8x24	3.0		6x32	5.3		2x42	21.0
9x24	2.7		6.5x32	4.9		3x42	14.0
10x24	2.4		7x32	4.6		6x42	7.0
12x24	2.0		8x32	4.0		7x42	6.0
15x24	1.6		8.5x32	3.8		7.5x42	5.6
6x25	4.2		9x32	3.6		8x42	5.3
7x25	3.6		10x32	3.2		8.5x42	4.9
8x25	3.1		12x32	2.7		9x42	4.7
9x25	2.8		16x32	2.0		10x42	4.2
10x25	2.5		20x32	1.6		12x42	3.5
12x25	2.1		7x33	4.7		12.5x42	3.4
15x25	1.7						

Exit Pupil = Objective Diameter (mm)/Power

Appendix B   Exit Pupil (EP) Size of Optical Instruments

Size	EP		Size	EP		Size	EP
16x42	2.6		30x50	1.7		12x70	5.8
7.5x43	5.7		35x50	1.4		14x70	5.0
8x43	5.4		36x50	1.4		15x70	4.7
8.5x43	5.1		40x50	1.3		16x70	4.4
10x43	4.3		45x50	1.1		20x70	3.5
10.5x43	4.1		10x51	5.1		25x70	2.8
3x44	14.7		12x51	4.3		30x70	2.3
4x44	11.0		15x51	3.4		36x70	1.9
6x44	7.3		10x52	5.2		60x70	1.2
7.5x44	5.9		12x52	4.3		100x70	0.7
8x44	5.5		16x52	3.3		11x80	7.3
8.5x44	5.2		3x56	18.7		12x80	6.7
10x44	4.4		8x56	7.0		15x80	5.3
10.5x44	4.2		8.5x56	6.6		16x80	5.0
12x44	3.7		10x56	5.6		18x80	4.4
16x44	2.8		11x56	5.1		20x80	4.0
18x44	2.4		12x56	4.7		25x80	3.2
8x45	5.6		13x56	4.3		30x80	2.7
8.5x45	5.3		15x56	3.7		36x80	2.2
10.5x45	4.3		32x56	1.8		40x80	2.0
11x45	4.1		9x60	6.7		52x80	1.5
12x45	3.8		10x60	6.0		60x80	1.3
15x45	3.0		12x60	5.0		125x80	0.6
3x50	16.7		15x60	4.0		140x80	0.6
4x50	12.5		20x60	3.0		20x82	4.1
6x50	8.3		30x60	2.0		32x82	2.6
7x50	7.1		40x60	1.5		60x82	1.4
8x50	6.3		45x60	1.3		20x85	4.3
8.5x50	5.9		50x60	1.2		60x85	1.4
9x50	5.6		60x60	1.0		20x90	4.5
10x50	5.0		9x63	7.0		14x100	7.1
12x50	4.2		12x63	5.3		20x100	5.0
14x50	3.6		15x63	4.2		22x100	4.5
15x50	3.3		15x65	4.3		25x100	4.0
16x50	3.1		16x65	4.1		40x100	2.5
18x50	2.8		45x65	1.4		20x120	6.0
20x50	2.5		48x65	1.4		30x120	4.0
21x50	2.4		10x70	7.0		30x125	4.2
22x50	2.3		10.5x70	6.7		25x150	6.0
24x50	2.1		11x70	6.4		35x150	4.3
						40x150	3.8

Exit Pupil = Objective Diameter (mm)/Power

Appendix C   Relative Brightness Index (RBI)

Size	RBI		Size	RBI		Size	RBI
5x15	25.0		16x25	2.4		8x33	17.0
6x16	7.1		17x25	2.2		9x33	13.4
7x18	6.6		20x25	1.6		6x35	34.0
1x20	400.0		21x25	1.4		7x35	25.0
2x20	100.0		27x25	0.8		8x35	19.1
3x20	44.4		28x25	0.8		9x35	15.1
4x20	25.0		80x25	0.1		10x35	12.3
5x20	16.0		7x26	13.8		12x35	8.5
6x20	11.1		8x26	10.6		15x35	5.4
7x20	8.2		8.5x26	9.4		17x35	4.2
8x20	6.3		10x26	6.8		20x35	3.1
9x20	4.9		9x27	9.0		6x36	36.0
10x20	4.0		10x27	7.3		7x36	26.4
5x21	17.6		8x28	12.3		8x36	20.3
6x21	12.3		9x28	9.7		10x36	13.0
6.5x21	10.4		10x28	7.8		12x36	9.0
7x21	9.0		10.5x28	7.1		3x40	177.8
8x21	6.9		4x30	56.3		4x40	100.0
8.5x21	6.1		6x30	25.0		6x40	44.4
10x21	4.4		7x30	18.4		7x40	32.7
8x22	7.6		8x30	14.1		8x40	25.0
6x23	14.7		9x30	11.1		9x40	19.8
8x23	8.3		10x30	9.0		10x40	16.0
10x23	5.3		12x30	6.0		12x40	11.1
12x23	3.7		1x32	1024.0		14x40	8.2
1x24	576.0		2x32	256.0		15x40	7.1
4x24	36.0		3x32	113.8		16x40	6.3
6x24	16.0		4x32	64.0		18x40	4.9
7x24	11.8		5x32	41.0		21x40	3.6
8x24	9.0		6x32	28.4		2x42	441.0
9x24	7.1		6.5x32	24.2		3x42	196.0
10x24	5.8		7x32	20.9		6x42	49.0
12x24	4.0		8x32	16.0		7x42	36.0
15x24	2.6		8.5x32	14.2		7.5x42	31.4
6x25	17.4		9x32	12.6		8x42	27.6
7x25	12.8		10x32	10.2		8.5x42	24.4
8x25	9.8		12x32	7.1		9x42	21.8
9x25	7.7		16x32	4.0		10x42	17.6
10x25	6.3		20x32	2.6		12x42	12.3
12x25	4.3		7x33	22.2		12.5x42	11.3
15x25	2.8						

R.B.I. = Exit Pupil (mm)^2

Appendix C Relative Brightness Index (RBI)

Size	RBI	Size	RBI	Size	RBI
16x42	6.9	30x50	2.8	12x70	34.0
7.5x43	32.9	35x50	2.0	14x70	25.0
8x43	28.9	36x50	1.9	15x70	21.8
8.5x43	25.6	40x50	1.6	16x70	19.1
10x43	18.5	45x50	1.2	20x70	12.3
10.5x43	16.8	10x51	26.0	25x70	7.8
3x44	215.1	12x51	18.1	30x70	5.4
4x44	121.0	15x51	11.6	36x70	3.8
6x44	53.8	10x52	27.0	60x70	1.4
7.5x44	34.4	12x52	18.8	100x70	0.5
8x44	30.3	16x52	10.6	11x80	52.9
8.5x44	26.8	3x56	348.4	12x80	44.4
10x44	19.4	8x56	49.0	15x80	28.4
10.5x44	17.6	8.5x56	43.4	16x80	25.0
12x44	13.4	10x56	31.4	18x80	19.8
16x44	7.6	11x56	25.9	20x80	16.0
18x44	6.0	12x56	21.8	25x80	10.2
8x45	31.6	13x56	18.6	30x80	7.1
8.5x45	28.0	15x56	13.9	36x80	4.9
10.5x45	18.4	32x56	3.1	40x80	4.0
11x45	16.7	9x60	44.4	52x80	2.4
12x45	14.1	10x60	36.0	60x80	1.8
15x45	9.0	12x60	25.0	125x80	0.4
3x50	277.8	15x60	16.0	140x80	0.3
4x50	156.3	20x60	9.0	20x82	16.8
6x50	69.4	30x60	4.0	32x82	6.6
7x50	51.0	40x60	2.3	60x82	1.9
8x50	39.1	45x60	1.8	20x85	18.1
8.5x50	34.6	50x60	1.4	60x85	2.0
9x50	30.9	60x60	1.0	20x90	20.3
10x50	25.0	9x63	49.0	14x100	51.0
12x50	17.4	12x63	27.6	20x100	25.0
14x50	12.8	15x63	17.6	22x100	20.7
15x50	11.1	15x65	18.8	25x100	16.0
16x50	9.8	16x65	16.5	40x100	6.3
18x50	7.7	45x65	2.1	20x120	36.0
20x50	6.3	48x65	1.8	30x120	16.0
21x50	5.7	10x70	49.0	30x125	17.4
22x50	5.2	10.5x70	44.4	25x150	36.0
24x50	4.3	11x70	40.5	35x150	18.4
				40x150	14.1

R.B.I. = Exit Pupil (mm)^2

Appendix D   Twilight Factor (TF)

Size	TF		Size	TF		Size	TF
5x15	8.7		16x25	20.0		8x33	16.2
6x16	9.8		17x25	20.6		9x33	17.2
7x18	11.2		20x25	22.4		6x35	14.5
1x20	4.5		21x25	22.9		7x35	15.7
2x20	6.3		27x25	26.0		8x35	16.7
3x20	7.7		28x25	26.5		9x35	17.7
4x20	8.9		80x25	44.7		10x35	18.7
5x20	10.0		7x26	13.5		12x35	20.5
6x20	11.0		8x26	14.4		15x35	22.9
7x20	11.8		8.5x26	14.9		17x35	24.4
8x20	12.6		10x26	16.1		20x35	26.5
9x20	13.4		9x27	15.6		6x36	14.7
10x20	14.1		10x27	16.4		7x36	15.9
5x21	10.2		8x28	15.0		8x36	17.0
6x21	11.2		9x28	15.9		10x36	19.0
6.5x21	11.7		10x28	16.7		12x36	20.8
7x21	12.1		10.5x28	17.1		3x40	11.0
8x21	13.0		4x30	11.0		4x40	12.6
8.5x21	13.4		6x30	13.4		6x40	15.5
10x21	14.5		7x30	14.5		7x40	16.7
8x22	13.3		8x30	15.5		8x40	17.9
6x23	11.7		9x30	16.4		9x40	19.0
8x23	13.6		10x30	17.3		10x40	20.0
10x23	15.2		12x30	19.0		12x40	21.9
12x23	16.6		1x32	5.7		14x40	23.7
1x24	4.9		2x32	8.0		15x40	24.5
4x24	9.8		3x32	9.8		16x40	25.3
6x24	12.0		4x32	11.3		18x40	26.8
7x24	13.0		5x32	12.6		21x40	29.0
8x24	13.9		6x32	13.9		2x42	9.2
9x24	14.7		6.5x32	14.4		3x42	11.2
10x24	15.5		7x32	15.0		6x42	15.9
12x24	17.0		8x32	16.0		7x42	17.1
15x24	19.0		8.5x32	16.5		7.5x42	17.7
6x25	12.2		9x32	17.0		8x42	18.3
7x25	13.2		10x32	17.9		8.5x42	18.9
8x25	14.1		12x32	19.6		9x42	19.4
9x25	15.0		16x32	22.6		10x42	20.5
10x25	15.8		20x32	25.3		12x42	22.4
12x25	17.3		7x33	15.2		12.5x42	22.9
15x25	19.4						

Twilight Factor = Power x Objective Lens Dia. (mm) & Square Root of it

Appendix D   Twilight Factor (TF)

Size	TF		Size	TF		Size	TF
16x42	25.9		30x50	38.7		12x70	29.0
7.5x43	18.0		35x50	41.8		14x70	31.3
8x43	18.5		36x50	42.4		15x70	32.4
8.5x43	19.1		40x50	44.7		16x70	33.5
10x43	20.7		45x50	47.4		20x70	37.4
10.5x43	21.2		10x51	22.6		25x70	41.8
3x44	11.5		12x51	24.7		30x70	45.8
4x44	13.3		15x51	27.7		36x70	50.2
6x44	16.2		10x52	22.8		60x70	64.8
7.5x44	18.2		12x52	25.0		100x70	83.7
8x44	18.8		16x52	28.8		11x80	29.7
8.5x44	19.3		3x56	13.0		12x80	31.0
10x44	21.0		8x56	21.2		15x80	34.6
10.5x44	21.5		8.5x56	21.8		16x80	35.8
12x44	23.0		10x56	23.7		18x80	37.9
16x44	26.5		11x56	24.8		20x80	40.0
18x44	28.1		12x56	25.9		25x80	44.7
8x45	19.0		13x56	27.0		30x80	49.0
8.5x45	19.6		15x56	29.0		36x80	53.7
10.5x45	21.7		32x56	42.3		40x80	56.6
11x45	22.2		9x60	23.2		52x80	64.5
12x45	23.2		10x60	24.5		60x80	69.3
15x45	26.0		12x60	26.8		125x80	100.0
3x50	12.2		15x60	30.0		140x80	105.8
4x50	14.1		20x60	34.6		20x82	40.5
6x50	17.3		30x60	42.4		32x82	50.6
7x50	18.7		40x60	49.0		60x82	70.1
8x50	20.0		45x60	52.0		20x85	41.2
8.5x50	20.6		50x60	54.8		60x85	71.4
9x50	21.2		60x60	60.0		20x90	42.4
10x50	22.4		9x63	23.8		14x100	37.4
12x50	24.5		12x63	27.5		20x100	44.7
14x50	26.5		15x63	30.7		22x100	46.9
15x50	27.4		15x65	31.2		25x100	50.0
16x50	28.3		16x65	32.2		40x100	63.2
18x50	30.0		45x65	54.1		20x120	49.0
20x50	31.6		48x65	55.9		30x120	60.0
21x50	32.4		10x70	26.5		30x125	61.2
22x50	33.2		10.5x70	27.1		25x150	61.2
24x50	34.6		11x70	27.7		35x150	72.5
						40x150	77.5

Twilight Factor = Power x Objective Lens Dia. (mm) & Square Root of it

Appendix E Mil-Dot Range Guide – Distance in Yards

Target - inches	6	9	12	15	18	20	22	24	30	36	42	48	60	72
Mil Dots														
0.5	333	500	667	833	1000	1111	1222	1333	1667	2000	2334	2667	3344	4000
1.0	167	250	333	417	500	556	611	667	833	1000	1167	1333	1667	2000
1.5	111	167	222	278	333	370	407	444	556	667	778	889	1111	1333
2.0	83	125	167	208	250	278	306	333	417	500	583	667	833	1000
2.5	67	100	133	167	200	222	244	267	333	400	467	533	667	800
3.0	56	83	111	139	167	185	204	222	278	333	389	444	556	667
3.5	48	71	95	119	143	159	175	190	238	286	333	381	476	571
4.0	42	63	83	104	125	139	153	167	208	250	292	333	417	500
4.5	37	56	74	93	111	123	136	148	185	222	259	296	370	444
5.0	33	50	67	83	100	111	122	133	167	200	233	267	333	400
5.5	30	45	61	76	91	101	111	121	152	182	212	242	303	364
6.0	28	42	56	69	83	93	102	111	139	167	194	222	278	333
6.5	26	38	51	64	77	85	94	103	128	154	180	205	256	308
7.0	24	36	48	60	71	79	87	95	119	143	167	190	238	286
7.5	22	33	44	56	67	74	81	89	111	133	156	178	222	267
8.0	21	31	42	52	63	69	76	83	104	125	146	167	208	250

Appendix F Mil-Dot Range Guide – Distance in Meters

Target-cm	15	23	30	38	46	51	56	61	76	91	107	122	152	183
Mil Dots														
0.5	300	460	600	760	920	1020	1120	1220	1520	1820	2140	2440	3040	3660
1.0	150	230	300	380	460	510	560	610	760	910	1070	1220	1520	1830
1.5	100	153	200	253	307	340	373	407	507	607	713	813	1013	1220
2.0	75	115	150	190	230	255	280	305	380	455	535	610	760	915
2.5	60	92	120	152	184	204	224	244	304	364	428	488	608	732
3.0	50	77	100	127	153	170	187	203	253	303	357	407	507	610
3.5	43	66	86	109	131	146	160	174	217	260	306	349	434	523
4.0	38	58	75	95	115	128	140	153	190	228	268	305	380	458
4.5	33	51	67	84	102	113	124	136	169	202	238	271	338	407
5.0	30	46	60	76	92	102	112	122	152	182	214	244	304	366
5.5	27	42	55	69	84	93	102	111	138	165	195	222	276	333
6.0	25	38	50	63	77	85	93	102	127	152	178	203	253	305
6.5	23	35	46	58	71	78	86	94	117	140	165	188	234	282
7.0	21	33	43	54	66	73	80	87	109	130	153	174	217	261
7.5	20	31	40	51	61	68	75	81	101	121	143	163	203	244
8.0	19	29	38	48	58	64	70	76	95	114	134	153	190	229

Appendix G   Books on Birding

There are numerous books and field guides on birding. Below is a very short list, in no particular order, about birds of North America. There are dozens of books available covering specific regions of the U.S.A. as well as various countries and continents, etc.

- *"Sibley's Birding Basics"* by David Allen Sibley
- *"The Art of Bird Identification: A Straightforward Approach to Putting a Name to the Bird"* by Peter Dunne
- *"The Bird Watching Answer Book: Everything You Need to Know to Enjoy Birds in Your Backyard and Beyond"* by Laura Erickson
- *"Identifying and Feeding Birds"* by Bill Thompson III
- *"Bird Watching and Other Nature Observations: A Journal"* by Joy M. Kiser
- *"Kaufman's Field Guide to Birds of North America"* by Kenn Kaufman
- *"National Geographic Field Guide to the Birds of North America (6th Edition)"* by Jon L. Dunn and Jonathan Alderfer
- *"Peterson Field Guide to Birds of North America"* by Roger Tory Peterson and Lee Allen Peterson
- *"The Stokes Field Guide to the Birds of North America"* by Donald & Lillian Stokes
- *"Smithsonian Field Guide to the Birds of North America"* by Ted Floyd
- *"Young Birder's Guide to Birds of North America"* by Bill Thompson III

Courtesy of Brin Best
using Celestron15x70 binoculars

Courtesy of Tasco

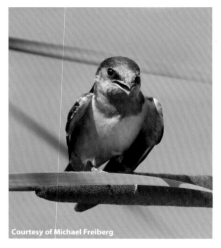

Courtesy of Michael Freiberg

Courtesy of Michael Freiberg

Courtesy of Bill Thompson III

Courtesy of Michael Freiberg

JADIMAGES/Shutterstock

Appendix H   Books on Astronomy using Binoculars

There are many books about astronomy as a hobby and specifically with using binoculars to get started. Below is a short list of some of the more popular books:

- *"Binocular Highlights: 99 Celestial Sights for Binocular Users"* by Gary Seronik
- *"Touring the Universe Through Binoculars"* by Philip S. Harrington
- *"Exploring the Night Sky with Binoculars"* by David Chandler, Billie Chandler, and Don Davis
- *"Observing the Night Sky with Binoculars: A Simple Guide to the Heavens"* by Stephen James O'Meara
- *"Binocular Stargazing"* by Mike D. Reynolds and David H. Levy
- *"Binocular Astronomy"* by Stephen Tonkin
- *"Stargazing with Binoculars"* by Robin Scagell and David Frydman
- *"Binocular Astronomy"* by Craig Crossen and Will Tirion

Courtesy of Damian Peach

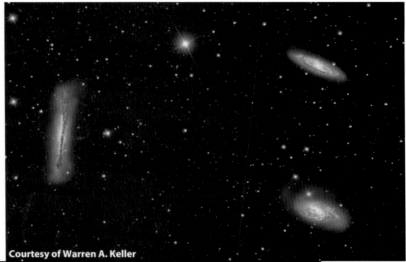

Courtesy of Warren A. Keller

JANUARY 11th, 2013
18:57:00 UTC (7 mins)

N

L p

Courtesy of Damian Peach

Eq Diam: 45.56" Alt: 76°

D. Peach

Courtesy of Tony Hallas/astrophoto.com

Appendix I   Books on Optics for Hunting

There are numerous magazines for hunters and a great many articles written about optics in them and online. I suggest you check out as many articles as you can to learn about optics as with hunting you will find that spotting scopes and especially binoculars are extremely important to your success in this sport.

Courtesy of Bushnell

There are not a whole lot of books discussing optics for hunting in detail but those that are available are quite good and the best of the ones I've read are listed below:

- *"Optics for the Hunter"* by John Barsness
- *"Shooters Bible: Guide to Optics"* by Thomas McIntyre
- *"The Gun Digest Book of Sporting Optics"* by Wayne van Zwoll
- *"Optics Digest"* by Clair Rees
- *"The Field&Stream Hunting Optics Handbook"* by Thomas McIntyre

Courtesy of Carl Zeiss

Tom Reichner/Shutterstock

Courtesy of Trijicon

Courtesy of Bushnell

© Aimpoint

Tom Reichner/Shutterstock

Julien_N/Shutterstock

Appendix J   Books on Target Shooting

There are many books available on target shooting. There are thousands of outdoor and indoor shooting ranges within the United States, where you can go as a beginner or as an advanced target shooter.

It is easy to get started and many ranges rent firearms which is great as your investment is zero while you try target shooting to see if you like it. Some of the better books discussing target shooting are below and are helpful if you want to try this hobby:

- *"The Perfect Pistol Shot"* by Albert H. Teague III
- *"Shoot: Your Guide to Shooting and Competition"* by Julie Golob
- *"Practical Shooting: Beyond Fundamentals"* by Brian Enos and Kris Kunkler
- *"Rifle: Steps to Success"* by Launi Meili
- *"Learning Shooting Sports"* by Kathrin Barth and Breate Breilich
- *"Champion Shooting: A Proven Process for Success at Any Level – Vol. 1* by Ben Stoeger and Jay Hirshberg

Daleen Loest/Shutterstock

Courtesy of Shooting Sports USA

Teerinvata/Shutterstock

Courtesy of Shooting Sports USA

Bikeriderlondon/Shutterstock

Appendix K Binoculars – U.S.A. Imports

Historical Data – Units Imported by Countries with Largest Quantities

Data in 1,000 of Units   -   HTS 90051000

	1996	1997	1998	1999	2000	2001	2002	2003	2004	2005	2006	2007	2008	2009	2010	2011	2012
China	8,282	9,540	10,814	11,049	11,824	11,548	13,424	17,424	12,750	14,460	9,955	9,332	9,101	6,543	8,048	6,235	6,839
Austria	18	26	35	46	73	52	89	57	105	72	94	84	84	109	90	103	120
Japan	715	850	985	1,752	1,549	859	739	595	1,096	907	269	210	378	1,064	866	176	104
Germany	114	93	112	66	61	80	83	97	112	126	121	154	120	85	97	109	64
Korea	300	364	683	279	223	143	80	66	263	38	26	9	5	6	25	27	34
Hong Kong	568	723	462	725	696	690	869	1,155	1,818	303	132	140	71	64	12	30	32
Taiwan	171	174	99	174	131	138	539	368	350	104	36	30	57	4	12	108	30
Philippines	384	381	358	453	349	284	240	210	172	124	124	93	102	43	46	24	26
Ukraine	5	55	3	17	4	1	54	11	6	5	6	7	20	18	16	18	20
Belarus	1	1	1	<1	1	1	2	3	2	7	29	43	16	10	9	12	13
United Kingdom	16	38	35	5	14	56	15	9	7	5	22	11	6	4	6	1	11
All Others	281	311	252	558	166	132	152	77	101	144	104	136	80	186	173	56	72
Totals	10,855	12,556	13,838	15,125	15,092	13,983	16,287	20,072	16,783	16,297	10,919	10,250	10,040	8,136	9,400	6,900	7,364

Binoculars – U.S.A. Imports

Historical Data – Units Imported by Countries with Largest Quantities

Data in 1,000 of Units

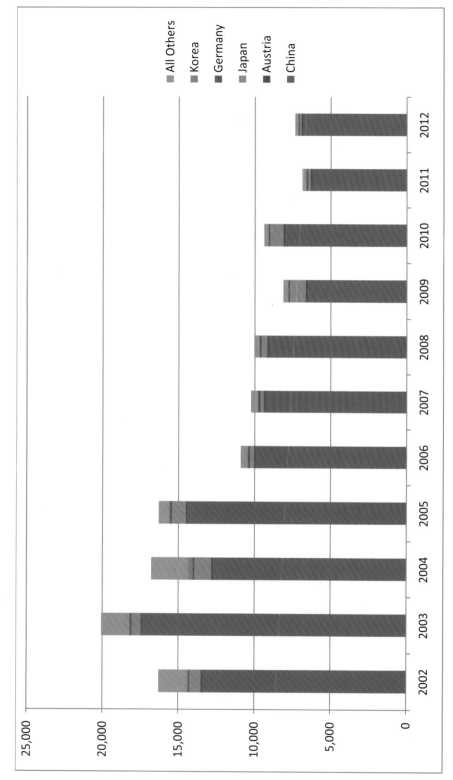

Binoculars – U.S.A. Imports

Historical Data - Imported Cost

Data in Millions of Dollars - HTS 90051000

	1996	1997	1998	1999	2000	2001	2002	2003	2004	2005	2006	2007	2008	2009	2010	2011	2012
China	61.1	73.8	81.4	74.0	77.0	68.8	83.8	99.4	105.1	84.0	89.5	92.4	98.9	66.9	86.0	85.7	82.5
Austria	3.5	3.9	4.9	5.7	9.8	8.0	11.0	15.6	17.7	14.6	15.8	17.6	12.6	9.7	14.8	15.4	20.1
Japan	34.0	34.3	32.5	37.8	39.6	32.2	27.7	22.3	20.7	20.0	17.9	20.9	25.1	18.3	18.4	25.8	18.6
Germany	7.5	9.6	9.9	10.5	10.0	15.8	16.4	18.4	17.3	21.6	18.2	19.8	16.3	10.9	12.5	15.5	14.0
Portugal	2.9	4.0	5.0	5.2	4.6	0.1	0.3	0.1	0.1	0.3	0.1	2.4	4.9	3.2	3.3	4.5	3.9
Belarus	0.4	0.2	0.1	0.1	0.3	0.2	0.4	0.6	0.3	1.3	3.7	5.1	2.6	2.8	1.7	2.4	2.7
Ukraine	0.3	1.2	0.2	0.8	0.4	0.1	0.3	1.1	1.1	1.6	1.2	1.1	2.4	2.8	2.2	3.0	2.2
Czech Republic	0.2	0.0	0.1	0.0	0.0	0.0	0.1	0.3	0.1	0.8	1.2	2.2	1.7	0.4	0.8	1.4	2.1
Philippines	8.1	8.3	7.6	9.7	7.3	6.4	5.7	4.1	3.3	2.3	2.3	2.1	3.6	1.9	2.9	1.2	1.3
Korea	6.8	9.0	11.0	5.6	4.4	2.8	1.9	1.6	1.6	0.8	0.8	0.2	0.1	0.2	0.3	0.6	1.2
Canada	0.0	0.4	1.1	0.1	0.2	0.2	0.5	0.6	0.3	0.3	1.0	1.6	2.4	1.9	2.8	2.4	0.9
Russia	7.4	5.2	1.9	4.3	2.5	1.9	2.3	2.2	2.9	8.7	6.3	3.1	2.3	1.3	0.4	1.2	0.7
Hong Kong	3.7	4.4	4.3	3.1	2.5	2.0	1.5	1.9	3.4	1.7	2.2	0.9	0.8	1.1	0.7	0.4	0.6
All Others	4.7	4.5	7.2	12.1	6.4	4.5	12.3	14.6	11.1	8.2	7.2	7.3	6.4	7.8	6.0	5.6	3.2
Totals	140.7	158.9	167.4	169.1	164.8	142.9	164.1	182.7	184.9	166.3	167.4	176.6	180.2	129.0	152.6	165.1	154.0

Binoculars – U.S.A. Imports

Historical Data - Imported Cost

Data in Millions of Dollars

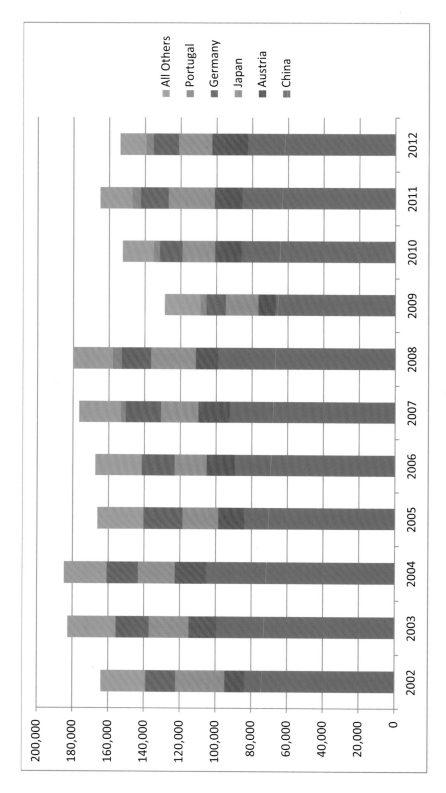

Appendix L   Riflescopes – U.S.A. Imports

Historical Data - Imported Cost including Tariff Charge

In 1,000 of U.S. Dollars — HTS - 90131010

Country	1996	1997	1998	1999	2000	2001	2002	2003	2004	2005	2006	2007	2008	2009	2010	2011	2012
Philippines	6,210	5,547	8,447	13,318	11,307	12,241	10,135	19,859	21,715	16,160	27,992	42,489	38,932	28,863	30,659	37,706	64,741
China	12,253	17,669	18,406	25,224	27,167	24,667	24,129	28,672	23,094	23,132	34,375	38,981	30,311	42,484	42,176	46,032	62,084
Japan	8,517	7,393	8,323	11,430	15,772	11,414	12,673	19,802	15,147	14,191	12,957	17,512	21,371	24,009	22,405	33,830	37,248
Germany	1,334	997	1,267	1,496	1,832	1,386	1,545	2,087	2,172	2,345	3,484	3,257	4,152	6,676	2,867	5,884	9,653
Korea	7,094	7,958	9,478	11,207	8,541	4,157	5,614	5,501	5,417	3,466	1,635	1,698	1,899	1,641	5,173	5,755	5,758
Canada	0	0	0	18	45	102	216	316	322	63	149	916	1,110	1,483	1,512	1,700	4,736
Austria	2,312	853	1,381	838	1,825	2,349	1,779	3,538	2,902	2,645	3,329	4,592	3,466	4,005	1,739	3,211	2,838
Czech Republic	0	0	66	63	36	14	90	51	6	167	159	286	389	79	309	744	1,223
Russia	7	2	31	317	191	209	87	15	101	198	52	0	77	568	324	306	898
Belgium	0	0	0	0	130	0	0	0	0	0	0	0	0	0	0	0	334
Taiwan	2,130	3,650	3,262	3,866	1,489	73	66	325	185	0	55	185	300	49	0	340	333
Romania	14	70	112	145	227	327	391	548	784	634	987	792	762	463	0	0	229
Hong Kong	248	145	730	355	0	10	4	233	32	3	52	161	27	168	63	380	88
United Kingdom	16	11	225	215	33	5	5	5	28	40	86	162	210	50	125	11	49
Israel	1,187	235	58	227	3	37	785	2,134	2,096	2,967	4,401	2,949	251	0	50	29	27
Subtotal :	41,323	44,529	51,786	68,720	68,597	56,990	57,520	83,084	73,999	66,010	89,713	113,978	103,259	110,538	107,403	135,928	190,240
All Other:	2,640	3,881	2,620	4,136	2,487	1,866	250	1,514	308	769	473	160	5,368	256	302	639	68
Total	43,963	48,410	54,406	72,856	71,084	58,856	57,770	84,598	74,307	66,779	90,186	114,139	108,627	110,794	107,705	136,567	190,308

Riflescope – U.S.A. Imports

Historical Data – Imported Cost Including Tariff Charge

In 1,000 dollars showing the largest imports by country

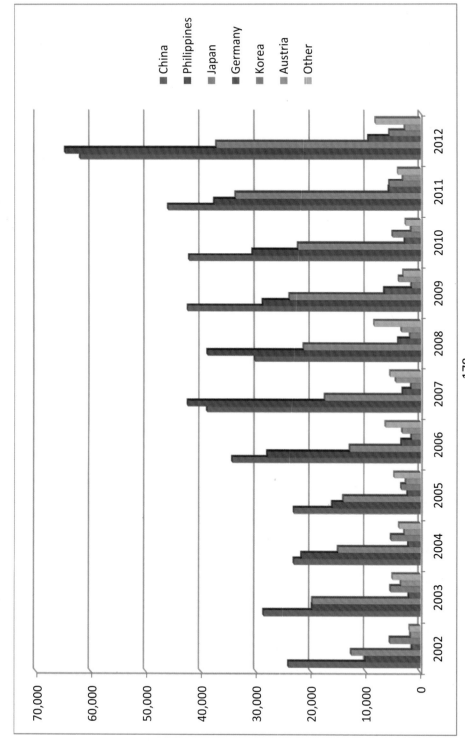

178

Riflescopes – U.S.A. Imports

Historical Data – Units Imported by Countries with Largest Quantities

HTS - 90131010

Data in 1,000 of Units

	1996	1997	1998	1999	2000	2001	2002	2003	2004	2005	2006	2007	2008	2009	2010	2011	2012
China	1,188	1,628	1,513	2,004	1,850	1,629	1,989	2,503	2,371	2,094	2,521	2,374	1,896	2,183	2,290	2,266	2,802
Philippines	136	123	163	238	212	174	150	286	408	259	344	447	418	368	428	508	810
Korea	231	233	276	310	224	102	148	172	145	79	43	41	49	32	117	132	139
Japan	130	94	103	104	124	1,055	116	185	146	110	104	125	119	141	97	118	132
Hong Kong	28	11	77	38	0	1	<1	21	1	1	2	45	2	3	2	8	8
Germany	2	2	2	3	6	3	3	5	4	3	7	4	4	19	4	14	7
Canada	0	0	0	<1	<1	<1	2	<1	5	>1	<1	1	9	1	4	2	5
Austria	4	2	3	4	4	5	3	5	3	3	4	5	4	4	1	3	2
Czech Republic	0	0	<1	1	<1	1	<1	1	<1	1	1	1	1	<1	1	2	2
Taiwan	46	85	67	61	23	1	1	6	3	0	1	14	13	1	0	3	2
Russia	<1	<1	1	5	2	2	1	<1	<1	<1	<1	0	<1	1	1	<1	1
Belgium	0	0	0	0	2	0	0	0	0	0	0	0	0	0	0	0	<1
Romania	<1	<1	1	1	1	1	1	2	3	2	3	2	1	1	0	0	<1
Turkey	0	0	0	0	0	0	0	0	0	0	<1	0	0	0	0	0	<1
United Kingdom	1	<1	<1	5	<1	1	<1	<1	<1	<1	1	1	1	<1	1	<1	<1
All Others	88	38	43	54	24	58	75	233	207	276	410	283	69	5	13	147	1
Totals	1,855	2,214	2,248	2,828	2,473	3,032	2,488	3,418	3,297	2,829	3,441	3,342	2,586	2,760	2,961	3,202	3,913

Riflescopes – U.S.A. Imports

Historical Data – Units Imported by Largest Countries – data in 1000 of units

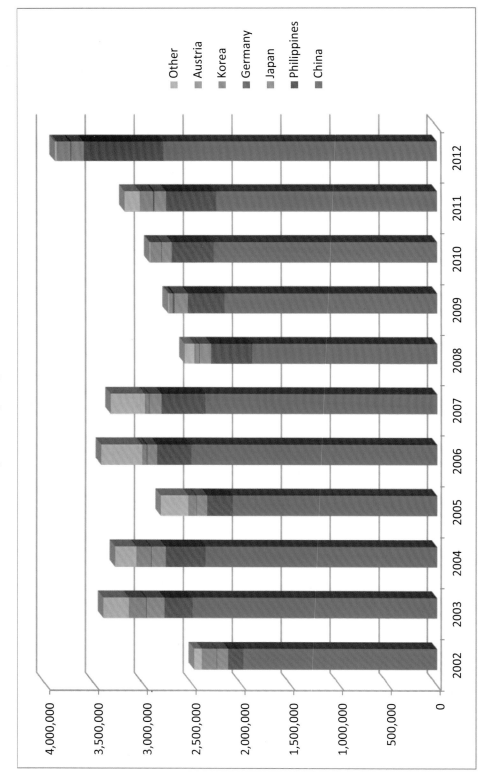

Summary

I hope you enjoyed reading this book and gained some new knowledge about sport optics products.

I tried, and I hope successfully, to have you open your mind and expand into other hobbies and areas with your optics product. As pointed out, you have so much to choose from in our fantastic world and enjoy it as much as you can.

Any comments about the book would be most helpful and much appreciated. I especially want to hear about any errors you may find so that they can be corrected in any updated revisions to the book.

You can contact me by email: 57ahale@gmail.com

Send postal mail:
    Alan Hale
    Hale Optics
    904 Silver Spur Road, # 191
    Rolling Hills Estates, CA90274 U.S.A.

About the Author

Alan R. Hale was the President and C.E.O. of Celestron for many years, as well as a minority owner in the past, and currently is Chairman Emeritus of Celestron.

Celestron is an international company and Hale was instrumental in leading it to be one of the world's largest optics manufacturers offering various optical products such as telescopes, binoculars, spotting scopes, microscopes, and related products.

Alan has been in the optical industry for over 50 years and has gained a vast knowledge of optical products and the various industry segments. He intimately knows and understands the sales and marketing environment of the wholesale and retail marketplace for astronomical telescopes as well as sport optics.

Alan has received B.S. and M.B.A. degrees. He passed the State of California CPA exam. Awarded Citation for Asteroid 13410 Arhale, discovered by Catalina Sky Survey in 1999 reads: "joined with Tom Johnson in the mid-1960s in the creation and development of the Schmidt-Cassegrain telescope and its ultimate production. In this, he was instrumental in bringing astronomy to many schools and ordinary people over the years.

He is an amateur bird watcher, an amateur astronomer, a casual hunter, a casual target shooter, a soccer coach, and an avid sports enthusiast. He is an active hiker and greatly enjoys nature and wildlife. In his spare time, Alan works on classic cars and currently owns a 1957 Chevrolet 2-dr Bel-Air Hardtop

He currently lives in Rancho Palos Verdes, California.